Amazing Face Reading

*Our faces provide a clear
and accurate mirror of
our life experiences.*
— Mac Fulfer

*Face Reading can change
your life because it will
change the way you see
and understand people.*

— *Mac Fulfer*

Amazing Face Reading

An Illustrated Encyclopedia for Reading Faces

MAC FULFER

Illustrations by Sandra Moore

Williams

Second Edition, Completely Revised
Copyright 1996 by Mac Fulfer. All Rights Reserved.

Website: amazingfacereading.com
Email: FaceReadng@aol.com

Copyright © 1994, 1996 by Mac Fulfer
First Printing 1994
Second Printing 1996, completely revised
Third Printing 1997, revised
Fourth Printing 1998
Fifth Printing 1998
Sixth Printing 1999
Printed in the United States of America

Illustrations by Sandra Moore Williams
Book design by Sandra Williams, Q Publishing Services

Library of Congress Cataloging-in-Publication Data
Fulfer, Mac
      The illustrated face reading encyclopedia: how to read faces /by
    Mac Fulfer.
      p.   cm.
    Includes bibliographical references and topic index.
    ISBN 0 - 9655931-2-6 : $17.95
    1. Physiognomy   I. Title.
    2. Sales
    3. Jury selection
    BF851.F85   1996

The author can be reached at:
      Email: FaceReadng@aol.com

Visit our website:
      amazingfacereading.com

ACKNOWLEDGMENTS

I have not attempted to cite all of the authorities and sources consulted in the preparation of this second edition. The list would include not only scores of published and unpublished authorities, but also all of the hundreds of friends and students who have taken the Amazing Face Reading classes and made valuable observations or shared personal insights and life stories that validated the material. Without their assistance this book would not have been possible.

I would also like to express my deepest appreciation for Pati Sophia, who illustrated the first edition. She had numerous helpful suggestions and was my true inspiration for taking on the task of writing a book. I must reserve a special acknowledgment for Janice Raoul who weathered Texas heat, pouring rain, freezing cold, and blinding wind as we set up our booth at weekend festivals and shows where I first hung up my sign, "Face Reading . . . Guaranteed." She provided space in her shop, The Rainbow Bridge, for the face reading laboratory where many of the classes have been held, and also proofed my book again and again without complaint. I want to thank my colleague, Diane Wanger, and my sister, Ronda Fulfer, both of whom helped me meet the deadline for the section on Jury Selection, which was presented originally as a seminar for the El Paso Bar and Legal Secretaries Association. My friend Patty Potter, who was one of my very first students and a very talented designer, deserves a special recognition for designing my brochure.

A special thanks goes to Dean Schlecht who wrote the forward and who has been a life example and inspiration to me. I want to thank Dr. William Ickes of the University of Texas at Arlington for his insights and observations.

Finally, a very special heartfelt thanks goes to Sandra Williams of Q Publishing Services, who spent countless hours developing the layout and production of this book together with hundreds of superb illustrations. I especially appreciate her patience with me as I made what must have seemed like unending revisions to both the text and the illustrations.

Disclaimer

This book is designed to provide information in regard to the subject matter covered. It is not the purpose of this book to reprint all the information that is otherwise available to the author, but to complement, amplify and supplement other texts. You are urged to read all the available material, learn as much as possible about face reading and tailor the information to your individual needs.

Every effort has been made to make this book as accurate and complete as possible. However, there may be mistakes both typographical and in content. Therefore, this text should only be used as a general guide and not as the ultimate source of face reading material.

The faces drawn for this book are from the illustrator's imagination and are not factual representations of anyone living or dead other than those so indicated in the sample readings. Any resemblance to persons living or dead is purely coincidental.

The purpose of this book is to educate and entertain. The author and artist assume no liability or responsibility to any person or entity with respect to any loss or damage caused or alleged to be caused, directly or indirectly by the information and illustrations in this book.

If you do not wish to be bound by the above, you may return this book to the author for a full refund.

CONTENTS

TOPIC INDEX

FOREWORD

There have been many things mankind knew, but did not understand until recently. For example, we've known forever that certain herbs have healing properties and that subtle atmospheric changes often presage significant changes in weather. Similarly, one of our most widely held, common-sense assumptions is that a person's character is revealed in his or her face. Abraham Lincoln commented that we may not be responsible for how we look when we are born, but our face at 50 bears the record of a lifetime of choices.

Emotions, temperament, attitudes and potentials all show through on our faces. How it works is only beginning to be understood. Leslie Brother's research on the universal connection between major emotions and certain facial expressions is a highly regarded study that helps validate what we have all already unconsciously assumed to be true*.

Every culture ever studied knew how to make extensive and frequently sophisticated use of herbal remedies long before anyone had the faintest idea why they worked. Likewise, we devote a great deal of attention and brain power to reading each other's faces. The more accurate our perceptions, the greater advantage we will have socially. Like the physical health of primitive peoples, our social well-being depends upon the careful utilization of a scientifically unproved, but time-tested body of knowledge.

Of the many kinds of human intelligence, emotional intelligence and the social awareness it brings, is the primary determinant of personal success according to Daniel Goleman, PhD. We live in an intricate, ever-changing web of human relationships. Negotiating the twists and turns of that web successfully depends upon how well we understand those who play pivotal roles in our lives.

Mac Fulfer's observations give us a succinct, comprehensible instrument for consciously expanding a fundamental skill we have all depended upon since

---

* "A Biological Perspective on Empathy," American Journal of Psychiatry,
   Vol. 146, page 1 (1989)

infancy: face reading. We all instinctively depend upon what we see in another's face for a major portion of our conscious and unconscious intuitions regarding another's temperament, feelings and intentions.

By analyzing and categorizing this intuitive knowledge, Mac has made a significant contribution to our ever-increasing need to improve our understanding of one another. He is like a modern day Linneaus in the domain of physiognomy. By serving as a translator for the body's most expressive unspoken statement, our own faces, he gives us a tool of remarkable potential power.

There are, of course, a plethora of semi-sciences and pseudo-sciences which make similar and even more astounding claims with little or no empirical support. Many of them are little more than "just so" stories. Their "successes" depend mostly upon gullibility and suggestibility. Their proponents seem cavalier in their attitude toward empirical verification. Often they seem more intent on establishing a doctrine than giving the truth of experience first priority.

This is not the case with face reading. Like the study of body language or spoken language, face reading is an attempt to attend more deeply to a pre-existing vehicle of communication. Mac has spent much time and study honing his observations and testing them against the self-perceptions of thousands of subjects. He is also currently pursuing the possibility of controlled scientific testing of face reading through a university psychological research laboratory. A telling marker of the validity of this methodology is that Mac has already gained local renown as an effective jury selection consultant through the use of his face reading skills.

People will go to great lengths to discern the truth about others. Knowing what the other person is truly like is probably one of the top three human preoccupations for obvious reasons. Any straightforward, easily-learned technique with that potential should readily draw considerable attention.

A special gift of face reading is that it gives us a concrete tool for helping protect ourselves from our own tendencies to block awareness of others through the distancing mechanisms of projection, generalization and assorted other defenses. Typically, we have a great deal invested in distorting social reality so that we can maintain our illusory, personal view of the world and of others. Any technique that helps us focus on another as a unique individual is a gift. As Mac once commented, "The fact that an effort is made to see and understand another person changes the interaction in a positive way. It builds trust and acceptance. It has changed the way I interact with and see people."

— *Dean Schlecht, M.Div., L.M.F.T.*
Author, A Way of Healing

PREFACE

I must admit that twenty years of practicing law has left its mark on me. I am skeptical of most of what I hear and half of what I see. Before I accept something as valid, it must be proven at least by a "preponderance of the evidence" and in some cases, "beyond a reasonable doubt."

Consequently, when I first heard of physiognomy, which is the scientific name for face reading, I was curious and interested but needed more proof. Initially, I read all that I could find on the topic and discovered that a lot of the material was obscure at best and sometimes erroneous. Many of the books I found were more than fifty years old and they reflected the attitudes of the society at that time.

After making copious notes on what I read, I wanted to test this information. To do that, I needed the opportunity to read many faces. So, I started a small arts and crafts business with a friend of mine, and for more than two years we spent weekends setting up our booth at more festivals, art shows, fairs, and celebrations than I care to remember. At these events, I hung out a sign that read, "Face Reading Guaranteed," and I read hundreds of faces.

I guaranteed that if the reading was not accurate, it was free. This improved my chances of honest feedback. In this way, I began to validate the information and develop my own knowledge and understanding. The feedback was incredible. After a while, I changed my sign to "Amazing Face Reading" because the response I most often heard was, "That was amazing, how do you do that?"

People began to ask me to speak to their companies, organizations, and professional groups. They also asked me to teach classes. The realtors at Wm. Rigg were interested in improving their sales. Members of the North Texas Romance Writers Guild wanted to make the characters in their books more believable. The Zales Jewelry loss prevention managers wanted to conduct better criminal investigation interviews. The managers at Mrs. Baird's Bakery were interested in team building. Members of the Fort Worth Paralegal

Association wanted to use face reading to assist in client communication. And the clients of Great Expectations, where the focus is on meeting new people, wanted to learn how to select more compatible partners in relationships.

I have taught face reading to high school teachers and principals, artists and photographers, psychologists and psychiatrists as well as doctors, lawyers, nurses, social workers, managers and even people in the media. Since its introduction, the Amazing Face Reading class has been one of the most popular classes in the Texas Christian University extended education program.

The old saying that you learn best what you teach has certainly proven true for me. In almost every class I have taught, the students bring a fresh insight, a touching personal experience, or an interesting new use for face reading. And each new group of faces has something unique to offer. This book is a result of all those classes.

Originally, I wanted to learn face reading to help in jury selection, but I now realize that face reading is much more than just a lawyer's tool. The potential applications are too numerous to count. My training as an attorney has taught me that words from a person's mouth are often the least reliable information I receive. Learning to read faces has been a communication breakthrough, and I have found it useful in interactions with all people. In fact, before I go to court, I read my face to check out my own non-verbal communication.

When I said at the beginning that twenty years of practicing law has left its mark on me, I was not kidding. I can actually see the results of practicing law etched in the features of my face: my mouth turns down at the corners which says among other things, that I tend to be skeptical about what people tell me.

You can discover what your face says, too. Your face is a living history of your life, and it may be one of the most intriguing things you'll ever read.

INTRODUCTION

"God has given you one face, and you make yourself another."
— *William Shakespeare*

What Is Face Reading?

The typical response to a face reading is: "That's incredible." "How did you do that?" "Are you psychic?" Most people will overlook the obvious answer. The answer is, "It is written on your face."

We all understand the importance of facial expression in communication. We know the meaning of a smile or a frown, but few realize that a face is a living record and personality profile rolled into one. Each face reflects in its structure and lines its owner's personal history, mental attitudes, character traits, intimacy requirements, work ethic, personal preferences, and much more.

A face can be read like a map that points the way to a deeper understanding of yourself and of every person you meet. And just like a map, this information is available to anyone who can read it. Learning to read this map is a lot like learning a new language, but fortunately it's a language that we already know. Even as infants, we begin life by learning to recognize and respond to faces. Our earliest emotional responses and reactions are developed by watching the facial expressions of those near us.

Face reading is an inherent part of our nature. Before there was a spoken language, groups of early humans had to rely on non-verbal communication. For primitive man, survival depended on the ability to read the meaning in the faces, gestures, and body language of his fellow man. Today we still read faces even if it is just to recognize each other, and most of us also have an immediate impression of each person we meet.

Certainly we identify each other by our faces, but most of us don't have an in-depth understanding of what else we are seeing. While we may have an instinctive feeling about each person we meet, we often tend to discount what we feel because we have no proof that our instincts are accurate. Face reading gives you a vocabulary to quickly and accurately verify your feelings and intuitions.

As humans we are physical, mental, emotional, and spiritual beings. Each of those aspects affects the others. How we think and feel affects the appearance of our face. For example, if you place yourself in a situation requiring intense and long-term mental focus, it will often affect you emotionally. Your response will also be reflected physically in your face, most often by vertical lines that will appear between your eyebrows.

Even more amazing is the fact that our faces are also shaped by our environment. While it is true that our faces reflect our inner character, it is also true that our sense of self-identity often depends on the feedback of those around us. For example, if we are never told we are beautiful, it will be difficult for us to feel beautiful. Since feelings are one of those aspects of being that affects the physical appearance of our face, over time this attitude will be etched in the lines on our face. A close attorney friend of mine was shocked to hear this. She said, "Do you mean that if I am in an environment where everyone responds to me negatively and then I change environments where the new groups of people responded to me differently that my face would change appearance?" The answer is, "Yes, absolutely." If you don't like the way you look, rather than considering plastic surgery perhaps a more effective solution would be to change your environment.

In face reading everything counts. We already know that each feature on our face has a structural significance: eyes are for sight, noses are for breathing and ears are for listening. But we may not realize that each feature also reveals an insight into a person's personality. From a face reading perspective, eyes indicate wariness, noses are about support, and ears reveal independence. Every feature and every line on a face is a physical embodiment of the mental, emotional and spiritual patterns and habits of its owner. Your face is a visual metaphor of your life.

This book was created as a quick reference guide, very much like an encyclopedia, to help you locate and understand the map of the face. Each face provides so much information that at first you might feel overwhelmed. That's a normal reaction, but don't worry, if you can match socks, you can read faces. A good way to approach learning face reading is to concentrate on one feature at a time. For example, you may notice the eyebrows of people you encounter and begin by learning to recognize and read that feature. Being able to read even a few features will give you immediate insights you probably never had before. The amount of information gleaned from a face will expand as you become more adept at reading the features. I had one student who amazed me by learning my entire book in a week.

Using Face Reading

The art of face reading is a wonderful and powerful tool when used to create understanding and openness. It is a gift that enables you to deepen your communication with every person you meet. To be able to see, understand, and then accept another individual at face value is a privilege and an honor that needs to be respected.

From your subject's point of view, it can be a little unnerving for a total stranger to be able to see so much about them so quickly. Therefore, first and foremost, it is important to respect your subject. If the information is construed as negative or invasive or if your subject feels it is being used to embarrass or intimidate, you may encounter denial and even hostility. Be aware of this and proceed with that understanding, striving always to show caring and a willingness to listen to feedback.

I never try to impose a reading on a subject and I am always open to the fact that the person's self-evaluation should be respected. Listening carefully to the response from your subject is an excellent means of becoming a better face reader. It will improve your ability to express what you see and give you insights about the meaning of the slight variations in the features.

My advice is that it is always best to read faces with a gentle, non-judgmental and accepting attitude. In focusing on the positive, you can help your subjects expand their own self-awareness. While we all want and need understanding and acceptance, we don't readily accept even our positive qualities until they are seen and acknowledged by someone else. The insights you can give your subjects can be the word of encouragement they need for their own self-development.

I have also noticed in my classes that students first recognize and see features on other students' faces that are most like their own. We all tend to see in others what we know best about ourselves. So I would encourage you to be gentle in your readings because the face you are reading may actually be your own reflected in another.

History Of Face Reading

The practice of physiognomy or face reading is an ancient art known around the world. Some texts on this fascinating subject have been preserved through the ages, and it has been a part of Chinese medicine for centuries. It has been a facet of Western civilization starting with the Greeks, who studied and wrote about the relationship between facial structure and character. Hippocrates, the Father of Medicine, was familiar with physiognomy. Aristotle, in his addendum to *History of Animals*, discussed how to read a person's character from his face. He also wrote a treatise devoted entirely to the study of face reading.

The fact that these works survived demonstrates how highly regarded they were throughout a significant period of Western history.

Over the centuries, many noted western scholars have studied and valued physiognomy, including Galen, the famous first-century physician, Chaucer, the author of *Canterbury Tales*, and Roger Bacon, the author and poet who many believe used the pen name of Shakespeare.

The first great advancement of physiognomy in the West came in 1775 with the publication of *Essays on Physiognomy* by Johann Kasper Lavater, a pastor and poet in Zurich. His book, with its scores of superb illustrations and his rigorous effort to produce a classification system, was the first Western attempt to approach physiognomy as a scientific study.

Johann Kasper Lavater
Father of Physiognomy

Many followed in Lavater's footsteps. For example, as late as 1913, *The Encyclopedia of Face and Form Reading*, by Mary Olmsted Stanton, was published and well-received. It was an exhaustive effort to classify the meaning of facial features and structures. Unfortunately, her work also reflects the prevailing sentiments and prejudices of that time period.

The reason you may not have heard of face reading is due to the initial success then ultimate failure of another competing discipline called phrenology. Phrenologists believed that the shape of the skull indicated the type of mind and character of its owner.

Initially, the phrenologists, called "bump readers," enjoyed tremendous success and had a large following. However, the theory that bumps on the skull correlate with the development of the brain beneath the bump was disproven by scientific research on brain mapping. Phrenologists quickly fell from favor and were ridiculed as frauds and charlatans.

This led to a rush to apply rigorous scientific proofs to all the disciplines, resulting in abandonment of many other avenues of research and study, including such worthwhile studies as hypnosis, reflexology, palmistry and telepathy. It has taken half a century for these to regain respectability as legitimate fields of research.

What About Genetics?

One question I am often asked is, "Isn't the way my face looks due to genetics?" While it is true that our physical appearance has a strong genetic component, scientists have discovered that many of our personality and character traits also have a genetic origin. We inherit facial features from our parents as well as many personality traits. Face reading is based on the observation made throughout the centuries that there is a correlation between the structure of the face and the personality or character of the person.

Face Reading . . . From The Beginning

As babies we all shared similar facial features and similar personality traits. Most babies have the facial features described below. The face reading definition follows the description of each feature.

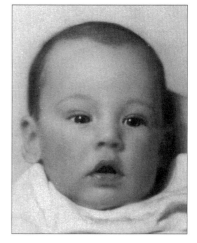

The author at five months.

Full round forehead . . . indicates a person who lives in the present moment and who uses what works best for now. We know that for babies, life is constant trial and error and this is their approach to life.

Large round eyes . . . indicate a person who is visually oriented and emotionally open to the world without being judgmental or wary. Babies experience the world by learning to recognize patterns and they trust easily.

Small, scooped-up nose . . . indicates a tremendous capacity for endless repetition and an immediate emotional response to the environment. This is certainly true of babies who always want you to "do it again."

Chubby cheeks . . . indicate a person with lots of energy. We know that when babies are awake they seem to be in constant motion.

Of course, our total personality is a combination of both nature and nurture. While nature, or genetics, plays an important part in the formation of our face, it is not the only factor. On the nurture side of the equation, we are marked by the major events in our life. Often, after a person has experienced a profound loss or trauma, new lines will appear on their face. These lines can appear almost immediately and serve as a permanent record and testament of their life experience.

We Are All Face Readers

On one level, we are all face readers. Most of us have an intuitive sense about each person we meet. Unfortunately, our vocabulary to describe what we read on another person's face is vague and limited. We tend to discount what we read on another's face because we have difficulty describing our intuitions. Therefore, we often ignore our perceptions, only later to realize we should have listened to that inner voice.

Instead of developing our perceptions, we typically fall back on our preconceived judgments and try to place the individual in a category that we can define. The checklist may include such things as gender, age, marital status, race, religion, occupation, geographical origin or social ranking. We determine what "box" the person belongs in and we may assume that he or she will have all the characteristics of that group. For example, I could be described as a single, middle-aged, middle-class, German-Irish, male attorney from Texas. Yet many of the assumptions you could make about a person who fits these categories would be wrong about me. On the other hand, if you could read my face, you would have an instant and accurate personality profile that would correctly describe me before I said a word.

In fact, psychologists have discovered that we learn to read faces before we can talk. Psychology experiments reveal that infants focus on and respond to their mother's face and her reactions to a startling event even more than they respond to the event itself. As infants, we mimic the facial gestures of those around us. Over the years, these habitual gestures become etched on our faces until they become a living record of our thought patterns and emotional responses. You could almost call it a living history written on your face.

If you want to become a face reader, you must begin by looking at faces. While this may sound so obvious as to be absurd, I have discovered from teaching Amazing Face Reading classes that we are reluctant to openly look at each other. Most of us in this culture have been taught that it is impolite to stare. The difference between staring and reading a person's face is that when we stare at someone, whether we realize it or not, our own face is revealing that we are judging that person and attempting to put them in their "box." If you have ever felt misjudged, you can understand why someone might take exception. However, when reading faces with an honest attempt to see, understand, and accept the other person as they are, the look on our face is one of recognition, which is not offensive.

Learning To Read

When reading a face, the first thing you will notice is that faces are not symmetrical. This knowledge gives a tremendous insight into the changes in a person's life.

When reading a face, the first thing I do is draw an imaginary vertical line down the center of the face from the forehead to the chin. Then I begin to notice all the differences between the left and right sides of the face (remember, it is not *your* left and right, but the left and right of the person being read).

Everything counts in reading, including the differences in lines, eyebrows, eyes, the two sides of the nose, nostril shape, cheeks and ears. The more noticeable the difference, the more significant the meaning. Scientists have discovered that the left half of our brain controls the right side of our body, including everything on the right side of our face. It makes no difference whether you are right- or left-handed.

Left-brain functions can be described as dividing the world into pieces of data, which we organize into logical sequences to predict an outcome. The left brain is the original personal computer, concerned with facts, logic, data, concrete thinking and linear time. This is reflected on the right side of the face. You could say that the right side of your face reflects how you take yourself out into your external or business world.

The right brain is concerned with non-linear or global consciousness. We can describe right-brain functions as our imaginative, intuitive, emotional, dream or childhood world, which is revealed on the left side of our face. We could say the left side of our face reflects our personal side or our inner thoughts and feelings.

An asymmetrical face shows that a person has one style in his personal life, but a different style in his professional life. For example, a difference in the "eye angle" will show a different approach to personal life versus the business world. If the left eye angles up and the right eye angles down, we can ascertain that this person is optimistic in personal matters and relationships, but tends to be pessimistic and guarded about outcomes in business and the public arena. Each difference between the left and right sides of the face will tell you where the subject approaches things differently in his public life versus his private life.

As you begin to study faces and learn each feature in turn, always keep in mind which side of the face you are reading for a more accurate insight into the whole person.

*"I have not volition enough left to dot my i's,
much less to comb my eyebrows."*

— *Charles Lamb , b.1775-1834*
English essayist, critic, and punster.

*"He's so narrow minded that if he fell on a pin,
it would blind him in both eyes."*

— *Fred Allen, b. 1894 -*
American radio wit.

*"I've always considered my face a convenience
rather than an ornament."*

— *Oliver Wendell Holmes, b. 1809 - 1894*
American author, physician, and humorist.

SECTION I — READING THE FEATURES

Seeing The Light

Light is not just a part of the electromagnetic spectrum. It is the reason for our existence. Without light, there would be no life as we know it. Not only do we respond to light, we become ill if we don't get enough of it. Beyond its physical effects, light is one of our most persistent and powerful human metaphors. We speak of being a "shining light." We often say when something is revealed that it has "come to light." Light is a metaphor for going outside ourselves and being willing to participate; to take ourselves out into the world. Light also equates with our desire for knowledge, recognition, status and power.

In face reading, it is important to notice how the subject's face reflects and responds to light. The way it reflects light reveals volumes about the subject's inner nature, and the way each facial feature reflects or responds to light indicates that feature's importance.

Each facial feature is uniquely significant on many levels at the same time. For example, on the physical level, your nose is how you take in air, which you must have for your immediate survival. Your nose is also a metaphor for how you sustain yourself. In simpler terms, your nose reflects your work life and how you give and receive support to sustain yourself and others. A very large nose that reflects a lot of light indicates a person who has a strong desire to make a big impact on his work world or who sees himself as a provider (*see page 27*).

Another example is a person who has very deep-set eyes (see *page 19*). To mimic the effect of having deeply recessed eyes, cup your hands around your eyes as if you were protecting them from the sun's glare. Deep-set eyes are a metaphor for protecting or guarding yourself as if backed into a cave. You may look relaxed and "laid-back," but you are constantly analyzing the external world to protect your inner world.

On the other hand, if you have eyes that protrude or bulge out into the light (*see page 19*), you want to be included. You eagerly sit on the edge of your seat to participate in conversation at every opportunity and your feelings may be hurt if you're not included.

Another example of response to light is an extremely heavy brow ridge (*see page 12*). The physical function of the forehead is to protect the brain. In face reading, the forehead reflects the style of thought. A heavy brow ridge on a forehead is the equivalent of a bill on a cap, shading you from light. If you have this feature, you generally want to know the "right way" to do things or the proper procedure or rule to apply. You have little use for theoretical and philosophical approaches that may throw more light on the subject but which do not produce a concrete decision or plan of action.

In face reading, chins reflect an assertive, competitive or aggressive characteristic. If you have a large or protruding chin that thrusts out into the light, you assert and project these qualities out into the world (*see page 51*). On the other hand, if your chin is strongly receding, seeming to hide in the shade of the rest of your face, you seldom project aggression or competition. You usually prefer compromise and consensus to assertive behavior.

As a final example, personal power is reflected in your cheeks. If you possess those light-reflecting, high, prominent, proud cheeks, you usually command attention as soon as you enter a room (*see page* 42). Your cheeks announce your arrival for all to notice. You may also experience an occasional uncooperative or even jealous attitude toward you on the part of others. The reason could be those powerful cheeks. It isn't uncommon for people to overreact to these symbols of personal power. These "Hollywood cheeks" can easily arouse jealousy in others at your effortless ability to hold the attention they secretly long for. In such cases, it is wise to remember to share the spotlight. We can all use a little light in our lives.

Once you understand the significance of a particular facial feature, you can gain additional insight into its importance by paying attention to how it reflects light or projects into or recedes from light.

On the following pages, illustrated variations of the features are shown with brief explanations of the metaphoric meaning plus keywords to help you remember what they are.

In face reading, the shape of the forehead can indicate a great deal about one's thought processes and problem solving style. It's not surprising that the forehead, which covers the frontal lobe of the brain, is an indicator of your typical style of thinking. For example, your style might be to seek a unique solution to each problem. Conversely, it might be a need to apply in the most efficient way what is already known or remembered.

Round and full (forehead protrudes forward)

- **Imagination**
- **Originality**
- **Dislikes rigid systems**

A round, full forehead indicates a desire to use imagination and originality in problem solving. You seek creative alternatives, and dislike rigid systems and procedures that limit your options. You prefer to be given the problem and allowed to figure out the best solution in your own way.

Backward angle (forehead slopes back)

- **Good memory**
- **Quick reaction**
- **Likes proven methods and procedures**

This type of forehead indicates a strong development of memory and quick mental reactions. You appreciate applications of proven methods and procedures to avoid wasting time. You are quick to apply learned facts and past experience to find immediate solutions. Once you've seen something done, you can often remember exactly how to do it and can usually do it easily.

Straight (forehead is straight up, no angle, not rounded)

- **Linear thinking**
- **Step-by-step**

You think in a logical, step-by-step process and have trouble taking information in if it is presented too fast or out of sequence. You need time to assimilate things and as a consequence, you don't think well under pressure. If you are pushed to think and act instantly, you may become overwhelmed and shut down. Your strength is when you learn something, you retain it practically forever.

Brow ridge (a bony ridge above the eyes)

- **Embraces rules and regulations**
- **Prefers certainty and known systems**

A brow ridge indicates that you prefer the "right" or proven answer and may feel immobilized if the rules are not followed. You appreciate the application of proven systems and like a no-nonsense, military-type approach. Once the rules are understood and accepted, you will generally follow them to the letter and expect others to do the same. For example, if a task requires a certain tool or procedure, that will be exactly what you use.

No brow ridge (no bony ridge above the eyes)

- **Flexible, adaptable**
- **Spontaneous approach**
- **Open to new ideas**

No brow ridge indicates a flexible, adaptable and spontaneous approach. In problem solving, you are open to new ideas. You seek whatever is needed in the moment and will use what works best for now. For example, if you don't have the exact tool you need, you will use whatever you have available. You avoid being overly technical and you resent being forced to be too exact or rigid in your approach.

Self-will pad (fleshy pad or bump between eyebrows)

- **Force of will**
- **Determination**

The space between the eyebrows is the area of self-will. When this feature is prominent, it indicates tremendous innate self-will. You can accomplish your goals by your force of will and sheer determination. Even as a child, once you made up your mind, you let nothing stand in your way.

The forehead ends where the eyebrows begin. What are these strange little patches of hair above our eyes? Your eyebrows are powerful visual cues that create a response in others just by their shape. There are three basic shapes with minor variations: curved, straight, and angled. Each shape reflects a different mental outlook. Even if you pluck your eyebrows, or draw them on, they still reflect the mental outlook that feels right for you. In fact, we can almost read each one of those individual eyebrow hairs as a symbolic representation of a habitual thought pattern. It may be surprising to notice that eyebrows are often different. The pattern and shape of the left eyebrow indicates our mental outlook in our personal life while the right eyebrow reflects our mental outlook in our external or business world.

Curved eyebrows (smooth curve)

- **People-oriented**
- **Connects and relates on a personal level**
- **Learns by example**

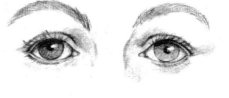

Your mental focus is people-oriented. You connect and relate to the world best through your understanding of people. Sometimes you can understand an idea or theory better if it is explained to you in terms of a personal example or experience. It is best not to burden you with too much technical detail without showing you a real-world application.

Straight eyebrows (no curve or angle)

- **Logical approach**
- **Needs facts**

Your approach is direct and factual, and you want the technical details. You appreciate logic, and you will need to be shown all the facts and available data before accepting something as true. You mentally evaluate the hard facts without letting emotion affect your judgment.

Angled eyebrows (definite up and down)

- **Needs to be mentally in control**
- **Wants to be right**
- **Evaluates carefully**

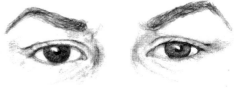

It is important for you to stay mentally in control of any situation in which you find yourself. Gregarious and expansive, you may have good leadership qualities because few people will challenge the authority of your eyebrows. You like to be right and usually are, having conscientiously "done your homework." You stay mentally focused.

Eyebrows

Position

The position of the eyebrows in relation to your eyes gives information about your approach to putting your thoughts out into the world. Raise your eyebrows and sense how your attitude is one of questioning. Then lower them as far as possible and notice how it fosters an attitude of intense concentration. These habitual attitudes are reflected on a face by the eyebrow position. If you can't tell yet whether someone's eyebrows are high or low, this is normal. As you study eyebrows more, you will soon know through experience whether they are high, low or somewhere in between.

High eyebrows (space between eye and eyebrow)

- **Selective and discriminating**
- **Wait-and-see approach**
- **Applies things to mental framework**

You are discerning, selective, and discriminating. You need time to observe and work out ideas completely before acting. You protect yourself with a wait-and-see approach. You need time to put new information on your mental framework. It is important for you to understand how you feel about the subject and how the parts relate to the whole. You store information with an emotional tab; by recalling the feeling, you can often recall the event with surprising clarity. You detest being put on the spot to make a snap assessment or to make a decision about something new before you have had time to reflect on it and understand it.

Low eyebrows (no space between eye and eyebrow)

- **Mentally quick**
- **Do it now**
- **Interrupts others to express self**

You are expressive, quick to take action and you process information quickly. You want to get the job done and do it now. You may have a tendency to interrupt others when they seem too slow to speak because you can often anticipate what they are going to say before they have finished saying it. You are initially optimistic but may become antagonistic if criticized. Your challenge is to develop more patience with others who don't have your gift of mental quickness.

There are specific types of eyebrows and each has a unique thought signature. Remember that the individual eyebrow hairs are symbolic representations of habitual thought patterns and are amazingly accurate!

Bushy (thick, full eyebrow hairs)

- **Non-stop thinker**

You are a mentally active person, full of thoughts and ideas. Bushy eyebrows can also indicate a powerful intellect.

Thin (like a pencil line)

- **Single-minded**
- **Overly concerned with opinions of others**

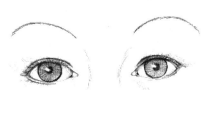

You are single-minded, focusing on one thing at a time. Your challenge is being overly sensitive to how you imagine others see you. You probably think they are more critical than they really are. You may sometimes feel overly self-conscious.

Winged (thick at beginning, becoming thinner at ends)

- **Visionary**
- **Sees big picture**
- **Dislikes details**

You need to be on the planning committee! You love coming up with big, new ideas. Your visionary approach allows you to create exciting new plans, but your challenge is with follow-through. Delegate details to someone else to free yourself up to focus on your grand visions.

Even (same thickness throughout length)

- **Even flow of thoughts**
- **Sees complete picture**
- **Attention to detail**

Your thoughts flow smoothly, evenly and you easily grasp whole concepts. Your challenge is developing a tolerance for other people's difficulty with detail. By your mental standards, the rest of the world may seem slow or even unable to fully comprehend ideas.

Managerial (thin at beginning, thick at outer edges)

- **Mentally organized**
- **Good with follow-through**

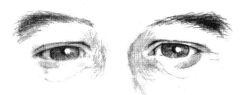

You may be slow to start something new, but once a task is accepted, you have great follow-through. Mentally tidy, well-organized, and methodical, you do well in any role that requires attention to detail and completion. You dot all the i's and cross all the t's.

Eyebrows

Continuous (both eyebrows connected)

- **Mind never stops**
- **Difficulty relaxing**

Your thoughts are continuous and restless. Your challenge is to learn to mentally rest and relax. If you have a problem, you may have trouble sleeping because you can't stop thinking. Meditation helps.

Tangled hairs (eyebrow hairs tangled)

- **Unconventional thinker**
- **Attracts conflict**
- **Sees all sides in any issue**

Your wild eyebrows signal that you are an unconventional thinker whose thoughts range over many areas. This gives you the ability to see all sides of an issue, and you may enjoy playing devil's advocate to discover hidden truths. Your unusual mind may also attract unwanted conflict. If you're getting more conflict than you want, try combing your eyebrows!

Access hairs (hairs growing straight up at beginning)

- **Inner/outer connection**
- **Can anticipate potential problems**

You have a strong connection between your inner feelings and your logical thinking. You have an ability to be aware of potential problems immediately. Access hairs on the right side indicate you spot problems in business and the public arena. On the left side, they indicate you anticipate potential problems in relationships.

Scattered hairs (single hairs at outside of eyebrows)

- **Curious mind**
- **Broad focus**
- **Many interests**

Your focus is wide ranging. You have a curious mind and are mentally drawn to many different topics. Each individual hair could almost be read as a separate mental interest. Your challenge is remaining focused on a single topic.

Chameleon (nearly invisible eyebrows)

- **Thinking style not obvious**
- **Blends into groups easily**

Your eyebrows do not give you away. Others may think you are just like them, whether you are or not. You can blend into almost any group and you may be a talented negotiator because you can extract more information than you reveal.

Since eyes are the primary sensory organ for light, it is no surprise that eyes have been called "the windows of the soul." Our eyes reflect our outlook, our attitudes, and our openness. Conversely, they tell when we filter or screen out information.

The shape, depth, relative size, and angle will tell a lot about how we approach life. The spacing of the eyes is about perspective. The average spacing between our eyes is about one eye's width apart. In reading this feature, only the very noticeable examples count. If you cannot immediately tell whether a person's eyes are very wide apart or very close together, don't read this feature.

Widely spaced (more than one eye's width apart)

- **Far-sighted**
- **Hates details**
- **Imaginative**

You have a broad, open perspective and a far-sighted imagination, but you hate dealing with details. You may be less grounded than most people and may even be considered "spacey" by those with a narrower field of view. Your challenge is gaining the financial reward you deserve for your broad insights, because compensation for your efforts is a detail you may overlook.

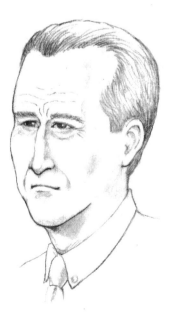

Closely spaced (less than one eye's width apart)

- **Good with details**
- **Extremely focused**

You are very focused on details and excel at exacting tasks where minute details are important. You do well in positions that require extreme focus, such as accounting, technical support, proofing documents and the like. Your challenge is learning to see the big picture and relating to others on their terms.

Eyes

Angle

The angle of our eyes indicates our world view and perspective. The eye angle will indicate whether we are optimists, pessimists, or realists. You can find this eye angle by drawing an imaginary line from the inside corner of each eye to the outside corner of each eye. Check each eye separately because they are not always the same. The right eye will reflect our professional or business outlook while the left eye will tell us how we view relationships and our personal life.

Angles up (outer corner higher than inner corner)

- **Optimist**
- **Inspired imagination**

You are good at inspiration and imagination. You are an optimist with a focus on the positive things in life. You expect things to turn out for the best. This attitude allows you to accomplish goals others would never try. Your challenge is to keep an even keel if plans don't work out as expected.

Angles down (outer corner lower than inner corner)

- **Expects problems, good at anticipating them**
- **Compassionate**
- **Admits mistakes**

You don't see the world through rose-colored glasses. In fact, you expect problems, and you are especially good at spotting potential trouble. You may find that others come to you with their problems because your eyes also show a genuine compassion for the suffering of others. You are quick to admit your errors and correct them, and you expect others to do the same.

No angle (inner and outer corners on a level line)

- **Pragmatic and objective**
- **Balanced view**
- **Resilient under stress**

You have a balanced view of life and tend to be pragmatic and objective. You are not easily discouraged and possess resilience under stress. If plans don't work out at first, you can continue on undaunted until they do. You are also concerned with fairness and justice.

The depth of the eye in the socket indicates your view about participating in life. The more "out-front" your eyes, the more willing you are to jump right in; the more recessed your eyes, the more you guard your inner being.

Bulging (eyes appear to bulge out of sockets)

- **Loves to be included**
- **Hates to be interrupted**

You are naturally enthusiastic and eager to participate. You don't have to run the show, but you want to be included in whatever is happening. Your challenge is that if you are interrupted, you may feel criticized and you will put up emotional walls because you don't feel appreciated.

Recessed (eyes are deep in sockets)

- **Reflective and reserved**
- **Cautious**
- **Observant**

You may seem calm and relaxed, but you are constantly evaluating everything. Even when you are nodding your head, it doesn't mean you are agreeing with what's being said. You question and weigh matters carefully and need proof before accepting anything. You protect your inner self by being reflective, reserved, cautious, and observant.

Eyes

Size of iris

The iris is the colored part of the eye and reflects metaphorically how we respond to the intensity of our environment. If as children we were exposed to negative, emotionally charged environments, as adults we often have small irises.

Large, full iris (seems to fill the eye)

- **Visual and experiential**
- **Responds emotionally**

You connect with your feelings and have an open, emotional response to life. You also have a visual and experiential approach and need to see the information you receive. You listen best when you can observe the person talking to you or see what someone is talking about.

Small iris (small in relation to the eyeball)

- **Allergic to shouting**
- **Needs physical reassurance**

As a child, your extreme sensitivity may have caused you to be painfully affected by people's actions and arguments. As a result, you may feel "allergic" to anyone shouting at you and hate loud verbal disapproval. You are more motivated by physical expressions of reassurance and acceptance.

Corner indents

Often, gifts and talents that they are unaware of show on a person's face.

Prescient points (light reflects off the skin beside the eyes)

- **Intuitive**
- **May anticipate events**

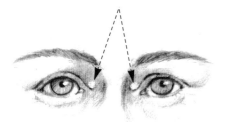

If you have these little highlights beside the bridge of your nose, you have an unusually high degree of sensitivity. They may appear as small, deep indents about the same diameter as a BB. You take in so much intuitively that you may be able to anticipate or have a foreknowledge of events before they happen. You also may have a natural empathic ability with people.

"The tombstone is about the only thing that can stand upright and lie on its face at the same time. "

—Mary Wilson Little - b.1880

Spotting Deception

When a person tells a direct lie, their pupils will slightly dilate for a split second. As a parlor game, you can test this fact by telling someone that you can read their mind as set out below.

Deception Exercise

Tell your subject to pick a number between one and ten and write it down immediately. It is important to get them to write it quickly. If given too much time, they may think of more than one number before making their final choice, and you may get more than one pupilary response.

After they have written down the number, tell them that to read their mind, you must get close enough to be within their auric field (or some other excuse). This allows you to put your face close enough to see their pupils and it keeps them from shifting their gaze. Then explain that you will ask them numbers, and each time you ask a number you want them to tell you, "No, that is not my number."

Of course, nine times they will be telling the truth, and one time they will be lying. On the one time they are lying, you should notice a slight pupil dilation. You may need to ask the number again to check your perception.

You need to remember their pupils will respond to what they are thinking and not necessarily to what you are saying. If you go through the numbers too fast, they may be anticipating that you will ask their number next, and you may get a false positive response.

With a little practice you can appear psychic. Of course, you are merely noting their normal physiological response. As I have said before, often the least reliable information we receive is what comes from the person's mouth, while what is often the most reliable are those responses that they can't control.

Eyes

Showing stress

Anytime we experience mental stress we also have a corresponding physiological response: our eyes "float" up. This appears as white showing between the eyelid and the iris, or colored part of our eye. Our eyes are in a constant expressive dance. With each even mildly stressful feeling or thought, they will react to indicate our true mental state.

Stressed (some white showing below iris)

- **Mental stress**

When the white is showing between the iris and the lower lid in both eyes, it indicates mental or emotional stress and possible fearful feelings or worry. If there is more white showing in your left eye, the stress is about concerns in your personal life. If there is more white showing in the right eye, the stressful thoughts or feelings are related to business, professional or financial factors.

Violent (white shows above iris)

- **Stressed to the point of possible violence**

If you see someone with the white showing above the iris, it indicates not only stress but also that the person may react in a violent manner. For example, a person who is approaching the psychological flight-or-fight threshold may have white showing above the iris.

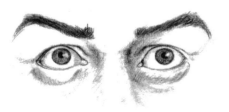

Disconnected (white is showing all the way around the iris)

- **Mental disconnect**
- **State of shock**

If you see someone with the white showing all the way around the iris, be careful. This indicates someone who may be in a state of extreme mental disconnect and may not even be aware of his actions. You will sometimes see this in a person who is going into shock after a catastrophic event or who is under the influence of dangerous drugs.

The skin that covers the eyeball is important for keeping out dust and particles, but it also serves as a tremendous source of communication. Our upper eyelids reflect our intimacy requirements.

Abundant lids (most of upper lid is visible with eyes open)

- **Strong need for intimacy**
- **Bonds with partner**

You have a strong need for intimacy. In relationships, you are a person who incorporates and bonds with your partner. You want someone who will consider you and share all aspects of life with you. For example, if your partner is going to be late, you want to be informed. You understand the meaning of commitment. Your challenge is learning to give your partner his or her own space.

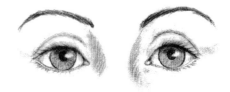

Thin lids (only a small part shows with eyes open)

- **Balanced intimacy requirements**
- **Can act independently**

You have a balanced intimacy requirement in relationships. You appreciate closeness, but are also capable of acting independently. You are a person who is neither a loner nor overly dependent. You appreciate intimacy, but you need your own space at least part of the time.

No lids (none shows when eyes are open)

- **Extreme focus**
- **Needs personal space**

You have the gift of extreme focus and need your own personal space. In relationships you need someone with enough ego strength to allow you plenty of room and not try to smother or control you. When you are focused on a task, you dislike demands from a partner on your time and attention. You are capable of intimacy when you are ready for it.

Eyelids

Bottom lids

Wouldn't you like to know if a person is open to what you are saying or if they are closed off with wariness, suspicion, skepticism, shyness or a judgmental stance? You can know a person's true attitude even when they are maintaining a pleasant smile just by checking out their bottom eyelids. When we are open and positive, our bottom lids become more curved to let in more light. When we become guarded or defensive, our bottom lids will become almost straight or flat.

Straight (bottom lids are straight across the eye)

- **Guarded**
- **Extremely loyal to friends**
- **Screens out information**

You are maintaining an emotional distance or self-protective attitude. You may be suspicious, fearful, mistrusting, anxious, or even shy. You keep your guard up and can be initially difficult to approach. Once you accept someone, however, you can be a most loyal friend, lover, spouse, or supporter.

If someone's bottom lids become straight while you are talking to them, the person has become suspicious and guarded. They are screening information through a wary, mistrustful mental filter. If the lid is straight on the left side only, the person is suspicious on a personal level. If the right side only is straight, the person is wary of the information being received or of something occurring in their external environment or professional life.

Curved (bottom lids are curved)

- **Open and receptive**
- **Non-judgmental**
- **Willing to listen**

You are positive, receptive and open to people and new ideas. You are willing to take in and want to consider all the facts and information.

If a person's lids become more curved as you talk, then he or she has just become more open to you and is truly listening to what you are saying.

Round (bottom lids are extremely rounded)

- **Emotionally vulnerable**
- **Very trusting**
- **Blunt**

You are extremely open and possibly emotionally vulnerable. You are trusting and sometimes naive with an almost childlike innocence. Your challenge is that you can sometimes be very blunt and lacking in tact. For example, in the fairy tale, it was such a child that pointed out, "the Emperor has no clothes!"

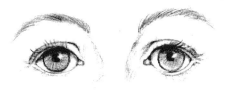

Eyelashes

Thick lashes (long and full)

- **Tolerant**
- **Gentle disposition**

You have a tolerant, accepting attitude and a gentle disposition. You are easy to get along with because you keep everything on an even keel.

Thin lashes (short and thin)

- **Extremely sensitive**

Because you are so sensitive, you may get your feelings hurt easily and be quick to anger. Your challenge is to learn to be more objective and try not to take things quite so personally.

Eye Puffs

On some people, you may notice loose skin above the eye that gives an appearance of "puffiness." If the skin above your upper eyelids appears to be falling down over your eye, you may be concentrating too hard on the external world while ignoring your own needs. You may be depriving yourself of rest, relaxation, proper exercise, or diet. Or you may be denying yourself any joy in life. These negative mental attitudes can cause you to feel uncomfortable or unhappy with your surroundings.

Moderate puffs (skin above the lids looks like extra folds)

- Impatient
- Overly sensitive
- Critical
- Denying self joy

You are focusing so hard on your external environment that you are ignoring your own needs. You are becoming impatient, overly sensitive, critical, and ill-natured. You would be happier (and so would those around you) if you paid more attention to your personal needs, including allowing yourself to have a little more joy in your life.

If the left eyelid is more puffy than the right, the strain and focus is in your personal life. If the right lid is puffier, you may be pushing yourself too hard in your business or professional life.

Intense puffs (skin above lid may hang down over eye)

- Ill-natured
- Defensive, selfish
- Denial

You need to develop a more positive outlook and avoid the use of drugs or alcohol as an escape. Heavy puffs indicate an ill-natured, defensive, selfish, and sometimes dishonest attitude. Your negative mental attitudes are not making you happy even when you are trying to convince others that you are.

You may have developed a negative, self-indulgent, or even jaded perspective, and there is a real need for a healing, mental adjustment. You may even be caught in a state of denial. If you are willing, professional counselling can help.

Located front and center, your nose is perhaps the most important organ on your face. If you have any doubts, try not breathing for a few minutes! Air is our first requirement for life. In fact, in some cultures, air is equated with spirit or the life force itself. Air provides the energy to sustain life and the nose provides the primary opening to receive this energy. The greater the capacity for taking in air, the more intense the energy. Since the nose is so essential to breathing, it should be no surprise that in face reading, the nose gives insights about how we sustain ourselves and those around us. Your nose not only indicates the amount of energy available to you, but also shows your work style and how you handle money.

Large (In proportion to the whole face)

- **Needs to be in position of authority**
- **Wants to have a major impact**

You have a great need to make a major contribution in your work. You are at your best when you are the supervisor, manager, or owner, because you want to have a substantial impact in your job. You are not satisfied with menial labor where you feel your efforts don't make a major difference.

Long (from between eyes to nose tip)

- **Needs to control work environment**

Your ability to control your work environment is important to you, including both the surroundings and the style. You operate best in a situation where you can control the pace and priority of work as well.

Short (in proportion to the whole face)

- **Gets the job done**
- **Hard worker**

You get down to business and get the job done. You are not afraid of hard work, and have an exceptional ability to handle the boring details that would be difficult for most people.

Nose

Long and straight (straight when viewed in profile)

- **Logical work style**
- **Long-range planner**

Your genius is developing logical, long-range plans and strategies. You lead the way in discovering new ideas and take a logical, no-nonsense approach to your work.

Concave ("ski slope" in profile)

- **Works from feelings**
- **Needs some acknowledgement for efforts**

Your feelings and emotions have an important impact on your work. In a positive, supportive environment, there is nothing you can't do, but in an emotionally negative situation, it is difficult for you to accomplish anything. You work according to your feelings and your work needs to be emotionally satisfying. It is also important that you receive some acknowledgement for your efforts: a simple thank you will often do.

Arched (curves out when viewed in profile)

- **Creative problem solver**
- **Mentally aggressive and practical**
- **Likes to direct others**

You appreciate beauty and elegance, but your real talent is in creative problem solving. You can usually see better ways to do things and are not afraid to try them. You are mentally aggressive and practical in thought. You are like an efficiency expert and you prefer to direct others. You like seeing your more efficient plans implemented and appreciated by others.

Bump on bridge (nose widens below bridge)

- **Feisty when cornered**

You can become feisty when backed into a corner and can be quite pugnacious. A frequent cause of this response in you is people who waffle on their stated position. If you get the other person to commit to his or her position before giving your response, you may avoid conflict.

Nose ridge

No ridge (flat space where nose joins face between eyes)

- **Team worker**

You do best when you can work with others. You enjoy working in a group where you can communicate and share experiences. If forced to work alone, you may feel isolated. Your talent is in teamwork and the ability to get support from others.

High ridge (distance from bridge to cheek)

- **Works best alone**

You prefer to work independently and do best when you can control your own work pace. You dislike having someone looking over your shoulder while you work (especially true if the ridge is flat down the center).

High, wide ridge (straight from forehead with no indent)

- **Iron will**

You have incredible will power and determination. You let nothing stop you from getting what you go after. This is the nose often seen on Roman statues, and it reflects the iron will of its owner. You turn your thoughts into actions with an incredible force of will.

Nose

Nose width

On each side of the nose tip there is a nose flange that covers your nostrils. The width of your nose at its base is determined by the distance between the outside of your nose flanges. Your nose flanges indicate how you give and receive support from others.

Wide nose (wide at base of nose)

- **Supports loved ones**
- **Willing to share**

You immediately give broad support to loved ones and extend this umbrella of support to cover and protect those close to you. You are also capable of receiving support and readily share with others, feeling that a part of your worth is in being able to be a provider.

Thin nose (nose appears pinched)

- **Independent**
- **Received little support from others**

You have received little emotional and/or financial support from outside sources and have had to pull yourself up by your own bootstraps. You are self-made and self-sufficient in providing for your own needs. You may feel that little was ever given freely to you. Your challenge is in receiving.

Crease (on flange)

- **Difficulty in receiving**

You have an independent "do-it-myself" attitude. While you give broad support, you have a more difficult time allowing yourself to receive support. It is easier for you to give than to receive.

Groove (a deeper line on the flange)

- **Extreme independence**

You have a fierce independence and may have been cut off from family wealth or emotional support. You often put others' needs and wants before your own.

Angle

If you draw an imaginary line running from where your nose connects to your upper lip and extending to the tip of your nose, this will show your "nose tip angle" as illustrated at right. The nose tip angle indicates your willingness to believe in others, and shows whether you are skeptical and mistrustful of others, or accepting.

Turns up (angles up in profile)

- **Spontaneous**

You can be impetuous in speech and spontaneous in action. You enjoy a good time, and you may find it hard to keep a secret. You are in touch with your emotions and live in the here and now. Open to others, you are willing to suspend your disbelief long enough to listen to their story even if they tell you about being abducted by aliens.

Turns up/pointed end (angles up with pointed tip)

- **Curious**
- **Spends freely**

You have an intense curiosity especially concerning people. Also, you spend money like water. Your attitude toward money is that it is like energy, "If I need more, I'll get it." It may be hard for you to hold on to money.

No angle (horizontal)

- **Solid and dependable**
- **Not gullible**

You are solid and dependable with good business sense. You are capable of extending trust to others without being gullible.

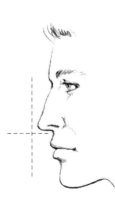

Nose Tip

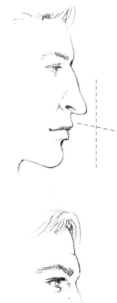

Turns down (angles down in profile)

- **Suspicious and skeptical**
- **Calculating**
- **Must be shown**

You are suspicious, skeptical, shrewd, and calculating, even toward those close to you. You give acceptance only after people have proven themselves to you. Your attitude is "Sure I'll believe you, but show me first."

Turns down/very pointed (downward tip has sharp point)

- **Ruthless**
- **Selfish**

Indicates possible ruthlessness, selfishness, and even dishonesty. If you don't believe it, just ask Hansel and Gretel about people with long, pointed, turned-down noses. Your challenge is learning to develop compassion and sympathy for others and their point of view.

Size and shape

To know a person's attitude about money, look at the tip of the nose. The bigger the tip, the greater the concern with money. For example, when the actor Karl Malden holds up an American Express card and says, "Don't leave home without it," we tend to believe him on an intuitive level because his large nose tip says he is aware of the value of money.

Big bulb (large bulb on the end of nose)

- **Financial security is important**
- **Collector**

You may have experienced financial scarcity in childhood and as a result, have a strong interest in gaining financial security, especially an adequate cash flow. You speak with authority on money matters and may also be a collector. Your mental focus is on acquiring whatever is needed to support your endeavors and pursuits.

Small ball (at tip of nose)

- Artistic sensibilities
- Appreciates beauty

You have a true appreciation of art and a need for beauty. You may even be an artist. You know quality when you see it. Beauty in your surroundings is important to you. You have an aesthetic approach to life.

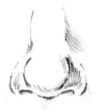

Skinny tip (thin, pinched tip)

- Free spender

You have little concern with holding onto money and may spend freely. Money is only valued for what it can buy. "Saving for a rainy day" is not your style. Your attitude is that life is too short to worry about money. This is especially true if you have a skinny nose tip and large nostrils.

Groove in tip (groove or dimple in center bottom of nose tip)

- Difficulty finding niche in life
- Job needs to be emotionally satisfying

There may be many times in your life when you question, "Is this what I'm supposed to be doing?" You feel like you haven't found your niche yet. You may be one of those people whose destiny includes many different jobs or pursuits, and you won't be happy until you've tried them all. Your job needs to feel right to you. You won't be truly satisfied until it does.

Heart shaped (nose tip looks like a plucked chicken's tail)

- Hard to be generous

The nose is flaccid and hangs down, appearing to squeeze the nostrils shut. Your challenge is with generosity — learning to openheartedly share with others.

Nostrils

Size and shape

The air we breathe to sustain life comes through the nostrils. The size of the nostrils gives indications about the flow of energy. It also correlates with how we spend money. It is also important to notice whether both nostrils are the same size and shape or different. Remember, the left side pertains to your personal or inner life, and the right side to your business or external life.

Very small nostrils

- **Thrifty and conservative**
- **Fear of scarcity**

Your friends may call you a "tightwad," but knowing the value of money, you are simply conservative and thrifty. Your challenge is that no matter what you have, you may still fear that you won't have enough.

Very large nostrils

- **Creative**
- **Generous to a fault**

You have a bold, expansive approach to life, sometimes throwing caution to the wind. You are creative and generous to a fault. Your challenge is finding limits.

Long, narrow nostrils

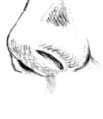

- **Emotionally generous**

You may be emotionally generous but financially conservative. You are ready to lend your ear but not your wallet.

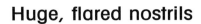

Huge, flared nostrils

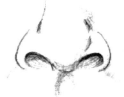

- **Intense energy**
- **Extravagant**
- **Self-confident**

You are self-confident. Your life energy is so intense that you may overestimate your own abilities and go to extremes. You want to be acknowledged by others for your achievements. Highly creative and imaginative, you may tend to think you are invincible and take on too much. You must learn to avoid excess.

Nostrils

Round nostrils

- **Generous**
- **Shares with others**

You are willing to give and are generous to a fault with both your time and money. You feel that you have more than enough resources for your own needs, so you immediately share what you have with those who are close to you.

Rectangular nostrils

- **Conventional, conservative spender**

You are a conventional spender who can stick to a budget. You are basically conservative in your spending habits.

Small triangular nostrils

- **Fear of not having enough**

Your childhood circumstances may have given you the attitude that there is never enough. Financially conservative, you may be a penny-pincher who holds on tightly to what you have.

Low septum (divider between nostrils)

- **Analytical**

A prominent septum that hangs lower than your nostrils indicates that you have good analytical abilities.

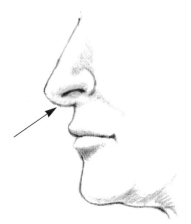

Ears

Size

If we call eyes "the windows of the soul," then our ears are the "doors" to our reality. Taking in information from all directions at once, our ears are our antennas, and the shape, size, and position of our ears reflects our personal reality.

Ears take in information from all sides, including directions in which we are not looking. They are just as important as our eyes for learning about our environment. We can easily imagine our early ancestors listening in the dark for warning of danger in the night.

Remember the left ear will reflect your personal life and your childhood approach, while the right ear will reflect your external world or business life. In face reading, ears indicate our learning style, or how we take in and process information: whether in an external, literal fashion or in an internal, intuitive style.

Large ears (proportionally large in relation to head)

- **Kind, receptive, and generous**

You are always ready to listen to others. Large ears also indicate kindness because one of the kindest things you can do for others is to listen to them and allow them to feel heard.

Small ears (proportionally small in relation to head)

- **Trusts in self**
- **Learns best when it can be seen**

Your focus is more self-centered. You trust in yourself and are less accepting of what you hear from others. You take in information best when you can see it.

If you examine your ears closely, you will notice that there is a ring of cartilage and skin at the outside edge that usually folds over to form a sort of cup. Inside that ring and closer to the opening of the ear you will usually find a second ring that may appear as a ridge. If the inner ring appears as a raised ridge or sticks out, it is considered a prominent inner ear ridge. If the inner ridge is missing or not defined, while the outer ring forms deep cups, then the outer ear cups are considered prominent. The more prominent the cup or ridge, the greater its importance to the reading.

If you imagine that logic is a gas that floats up out of your ears, notice how much would be trapped in the curve of the outer ear cup. If the outer ear forms large cups, your focus is on a logical, practical, and grounded reality. If those outer ear cups have gaps or if they are so thin that the imaginary logic gas would float out, then you tune in to a different plane of consciousness. You aren't comfortable with the mundane nine-to-five world. Internally, you connect with global consciousness, creative awareness, or a more spiritual understanding. If your inner ear ridge is detectable, it indicates you use some intuition in your decision-making process.

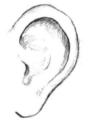

Prominent outer ear cups

- **Focused on outer world**
- **Logical and practical**

Your focus of reality is on the external world. You appreciate objective facts, numbers, and statistics. Your style is logical and practical, and you need external proof and data.

Prominent inner ear ridges

- **Focused on inner world**
- **Intuitive**

Your focus of reality is on the inner world and your feelings. You have a creative, intuitive, and highly subjective approach. Before you accept something as valid, it must pass your "gut check" and feel right regardless of how logical it may appear.

Clear separation between inner ridge and outer cup

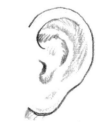

- **Good balance between personal life and business life**

You maintain a good balance between your private life and your work, keeping them separate so you have no trouble leaving the problems of the office at the office. You weigh things carefully before acting.

No clear definition between ridge and cup

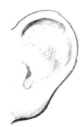

- **Egotistical**
- **Not practical**

You may overestimate your abilities and tend to be somewhat egotistical at times, relying on your internal desire or feeling without considering the practicalities.

Ears

Placement

Another consideration is the angle of the ears or how they are placed on the head. Draw an imaginary line through the top center of the ear and down through the center of the lobe. Is that line parallel to the angle of the face or at backward angle? The greater the angle, the stronger the trait.

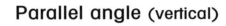

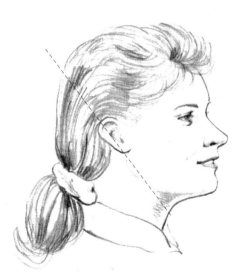

Parallel angle (vertical)

- **Operates from established norm**

You have a balanced perception and understanding. You are comfortable with the established norm.

Pronounced angle (slants backward)

- **Unique outlook**

You have a unique perspective and outlook on life. You definitely march to the sound of a different drummer and have your own unique slant on life.

Stick out (away from head)

- **Non-conformist**

You are an independent, non-conformist who tends to charge ahead. Your challenge is to let others know you can consider their opinions. If the left ear sticks out more, you are more independent in your personal life. If the right one sticks out more, you are independent in your external or business world.

Close to head (almost touch head)

- **Conformist**

You prefer to conform to known social values and can follow instructions. You are good at knowing what most people think. You don't like to appear odd or too different from other people. This understanding of the norm can be an asset in marketing.

Diplomat ears (tops close to head, bottoms stick out)

- **Diplomatic**

You take a diplomatic approach. You can see and relate to both sides, understanding both the non-conformist and the traditional view. You can express the middle ground between the extremes.

Ears

Height

High tops (tops are equal to or higher than eyes)

- Gathers information rapidly
- Approach is "do it now"

You have a mind that takes in information immediately. With an approach of "do it now," you want to see results. Your challenge is that you may overlook important details in your haste.

Low bottoms (ear lobes are equal to or lower than bottom of nose)

- Gathers information carefully
- Approach is "do it right"

You have a "do it right" approach. A patient listener, you may feel you will miss something if you are forced to rush. You prefer a slow, steady, and careful approach to matters and are always ready to hear more.

The relationship between the ears and eyebrows is one of the most revealing aspects of face reading. This indicates how we take in and process information. Look at the examples below and note the differences. See if you have an intuitive "feeling" about the face before you read the definition. *(Ears are high or low in relation to the eyes and the bottom of the nose as shown by the dashed lines. See page 40.)*

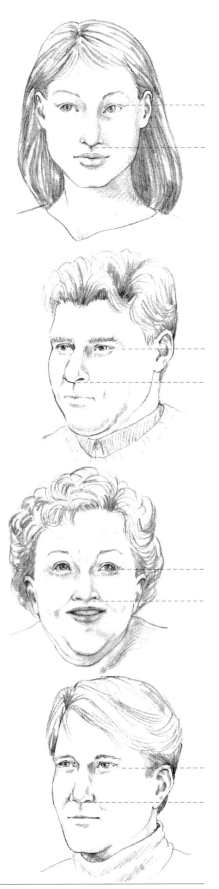

High ears/high eyebrows

- **Sensory overload**
- **Needs time to process**

You absorb information quickly and may take in more than you can immediately process. You need time to place new information on your mental framework before acting on it. At times you may feel a sensory overload from taking in too much at once.

High ears/low eyebrows

- **Instantaneous input and output**
- **Intimidating**

You absorb and process information quickly and can immediately express what you have learned, giving you a powerful and intimidating presence. Your challenge is to slow down and explain your thoughts and give examples to others who don't possess this ability. In slow methodical work, you may sometimes overlook details in your haste.

Low ears/high eyebrows

- **Patient, careful approach**
- **Logical, long-range planner**

You have the mental patience for the long haul which will often carry you further than the quick thinkers. You hate to be put on the spot to immediately say how you feel about something. Logical, long-range plans are your forté. A good listener, you take in the information you need to get things right.

Low ears/low eyebrows

- **Internal stress**
- **Wants it now and wants it perfect**

You may feel a need to express your ideas before you have all the information you want. This creates an internal conflict because you want things to be perfect, but also demand the results instantly. This conflict creates great stress from within. Some advice would be to ease up on yourself.

Cheeks

Cheeks indicate your personal power as perceived by others. Often the first response you receive from others is their unconscious response to your cheeks!

Protruding (the kind often seen on movie stars)

- **Power symbols**
- **Gets attention**
- **Others may be jealous**

When you walk into the room, you immediately grab attention as the light reflects from those power symbols you call cheeks. You are perceived as a courageous leader even if you don't believe you are. Your challenge is that others may be jealous of your ability to grab the limelight and may perceive you as having more status, power, or prestige than they do. When you encounter opposition for no apparent reason, it might be a good time to share the spotlight and acknowledge others for their contributions.

Full (rounded with no bones showing)

- **Gets broad support**
- **Excellent organizer**

Your cheeks are non-threatening, communicating a tolerance and acceptance of others. You are able to get broad support from people. You have no trouble organizing a group and getting people to join your parade. You are an excellent organizer and consensus builder.

Narrow (cheeks are high and close together)

- **Intense bursts of energy**
- **Hates working with slow people**

Your energy expenditure is intense but needs replenishing with occasional intervals of rest and/or nourishment. Your energy is like that of a quarter horse: you are good for short bursts of intense action and are great at meeting a tight deadline. However, you hate to work with slow people or in situations that plod along. You work best when you can take breaks every two or three hours, even if for just a few minutes.

Wide cheeks (cheeks are set far apart)

- **Endurance and stamina**
- **Great personal power**

You can go the distance because you have long-term energy and endurance. While you go at your own pace, you will often wear out most people who try to keep up with you because you never quit. You are in there for the long haul. Not easily daunted, you approach most tasks with a "can do" attitude and great personal power.

Sunken cheeks (cheeks appear flaccid)

- **Need to conserve physical energy**

This indicates a lack of personal power and possible physical illness or emotional strain. You are more focused on your inner world and intuitions than on the external world. You may need to conserve your physical energy.

Healer cheeks (broadest at sides, beside eyes)

- **Natural healer**
- **Uplifting presence**

You surround yourself with an aura of nurturing, healing, and uplifting energy. You would be a good doctor, nurse, psychologist, counselor, massage therapist, teacher, or parent. Your special gift is an ability to uplift and encourage others.

Mouth

Size

Of all the facial features, our mouth brings us into the most immediate and continuous contact with our environment. As babies, we instinctively put everything in our mouths to confirm its reality. Every bite of food we eat and every word we speak passes through this portal we call a mouth. This fascinating organ not only indicates our style of expressiveness, but also our degree of sensuality and even how we interpret what others tell us.

Large mouth (in proportion to face)

- **Extrovert**
- **Confident**
- **Expressive**

You are extroverted, outgoing and talkative, showing more confidence in expressing yourself than people with small mouths. The larger your mouth, the more outgoing and expressive you will tend to be.

Small mouth (in proportion to face)

- **Introvert**
- **Reserved**
- **Cautious**

You are introverted and reserved. You don't reveal your inner thoughts and feelings until you know someone very well and then only when you have thought about it. The expression, "still waters run deep" would apply to your approach to life.

Your mouth angle reflects how you listen. To determine the mouth angle, draw an imaginary dot at each corner of the mouth and one in the center, then mentally connect the dots.

Mouth turns up (when relaxed and not smiling)

- **Optimist**

You are an optimist in your listening. You always hear only the best in what people tell you. This is very rare, because most of us with any life experience do not enthusiastically believe whatever we are told.

Mouth is straight (forms straight line when relaxed)

- **Objective**
- **Reflective listener**

You are an objective listener. You can be a very clear, reflective mirror for others in that you are capable of reflecting back to them your realistic impression of what they have said without making it either better or worse.

Mouth turns down (when relaxed and not smiling)

- **Mistrust what you are told**
- **Prepared to hear the worst**

You may tend to mistrust what others tell you. The positive side of this trait is that you are not disappointed when things don't turn out as you were told, because you didn't have high expectations. The challenge with this trait is that you may screen out positive information about yourself such as a compliment, and you may hear the worst in what is said even when it is not intended. For example, if someone appraises your work and tells you it is "alright" or "fine," you may take that as criticism. If they didn't say it was "great" or "wonderful," you may believe they really meant it wasn't good enough.

Lips

Size and shape

The lips are the parts of our mouth that form the words we speak and the kisses we bestow. The upper lip represents feminine energy. (It is no surprise that men often cover it with a moustache to emphasize their masculinity). The upper lip also indicates aspects of our inner world including our feelings. The bottom lip indicates masculine energy, showing how we relate to the external world and reflects our focus on doing.

Full lips (both lips are large and full)

- **Emotionally expressive**
- **Sense of humor**

You are emotionally expressive and sensuous and may be physically demonstrative. You have a good sense of humor and enjoy expressing yourself at every opportunity.

Full lower lip (lower lip is definitely larger than upper one)

- **Can be persuasive**
- **Focused on outcome**

You have a "gift of gab" when it comes to convincing others of your point of view, especially about the external world of facts and figures. If your bottom lip is twice as big as the top one, your natural gift of persuasion allows you to charm your listeners into believing whatever you say. Your focus is on doing. Your challenge is learning to connect with and express your feelings. If your upper lip is especially thin, you stick to the facts and may even substitute fact for feeling in expressing yourself.

Full upper lip (upper lip is definitely larger than lower one)

- **Outspoken**
- **Expresses feelings verbally**
- **Perceptive**

You relate to the true character of others rather than what they say. You are outspoken and don't hesitate to "tell it like it is" when your laser perception senses deception in others. You question others' true motives. You delight in expressing your feelings verbally, but need to learn to be gentle with people who can be wounded by your insights. Your challenge is that others may mistrust your insights unless you can back them up with concrete facts.

Thin lips (in extreme cases, no lips show, only a thin line)

- **Cool reserved**
- **Mistrusts flattery**

As a child, you may have been held to impossibly high standards, and you may have been criticized or not sufficiently praised. You guard your feelings and opinions and are careful about expressing anything that would expose you to criticism.

You have a cool, calculating disposition. Reserved and cautious, you don't trust easily. You especially mistrust flattery and verbal expressions of emotion. Your challenge is to live less in your head and learn to express your feelings and emotions.

If you have thin lips and a wide mouth, you may be slow to start, but once started, you can be a good communicator with a wry sense of humor.

Cupid's bow (upper lip looks like Cupid's bow)

- **Get what you go after**

You have the ability to imagine what you desire and then manifest it easily. Somehow, you manage to get whatever you go after.

This gift of manifestation is easy to understand if you think about it. To manifest your thoughts or ideas, you first need to get others to listen. This little arrow on the upper lip acts as a subconscious neon sign, keeping the attention focused on your mouth. Women can accentuate this gift of nature with a little well-placed lipstick. This also draws more attention to the upper lip, which expresses feminine energy.

Teeth

In our dreams, losing our teeth may represent a loss of personal power or a fear about our ability to survive. In face reading, our teeth show how we make decisions and give some indications of personal strength and determination.

Even teeth (all teeth are the same length)

- **Logical approach**
- **Self-confidence**

You have a logical approach and learn life's lessons quickly. You make decisions with poise and self-confidence.

Gap between front teeth (space between teeth)

- **Takes risks**
- **Makes intuitive decisions in the moment**

You are willing to take risks even when you are not sure of the outcome. In fact, given a choice between playing it safe or going for it, you will choose to go for it. The larger the gap, the stronger this trait. Your friends may see you as something of a daredevil because you make intuitive decisions in the moment and don't hide from danger.

Big front teeth (much larger than other teeth)

- **Stubborn**

Once you finally make up your mind, that's it! You can be as stubborn as a mule and someone has to show you that you are wrong before you will change your mind. You have the ability to hang on to your position when faced with opposition.

Crooked teeth (especially bottom teeth)

- **Sees both sides**
- **Holds self to impossible standards**

You see both sides of every issue. While you might be good at debate, you hate to be wrong, so you will often double check your facts before proceeding. Your challenge is that you hold yourself to impossibly high standards, weighing every decision.

Buck teeth (front teeth protrude)

- **Had to overcome childhood shyness**

You have had to overcome the shyness you felt as a child when you would lean over backwards to please and try to get along with others. Your challenge is that you have had to struggle to become more outgoing.

A genuine smile is something that comes from the heart. Your smile reveals more about your true inner character and personality than almost any other gesture. A mouth turns up to smile. If it turns down to smile, it is a mask and does not reflect a sincere or warm greeting.

Natural smile (lips relaxed, full smile, teeth but no gums)

- **Comfortable with your sensuality**

You are comfortable with your own sensuality, neither flaunting nor hiding it. You also feel comfortable with your own sexuality.

Gums showing (gums show in a full smile)

- **Generous giver**
- **Questions own lovability**

If your gums show when you smile fully, this indicates that you believe you are desirable for what you can give and do. You may be inappropriate in how much you give, finding it difficult to accept that you are loveable for just being yourself. You try to earn love through what you give and do for others. You may be one of those people who wants to give everyone a Christmas present whether you receive one in return or not.

Lips stretched tight (upper lip tight across teeth)

- **False sincerity**
- **Hidden agenda**

This "overly sincere" smile is a mask that hides the owner's true agenda with an attempt to communicate an unfelt sincerity or caring. It is a deception flashed to make an impression. Be careful about buying a used car from a person with this smile!

Lips together (pursed lips or "kissy" smile)

- **Wants space**

You are communicating that you want to maintain your distance. Your smile says, "I'm being polite, don't rush me. It takes time to get to know me, but don't stop trying."

Crooked smile (one side higher than the other)

- **Performance smile**

You have a practiced performance smile that is designed to make a good impression but doesn't reflect your true feelings. You may just be smiling for the camera.

Jaws

Jaws show physical power, determination and strength. The bigger the jaws, the greater the physical stamina. Always check to see if one jaw is bigger than the other. If the right jaw is bigger, the person has developed greater stamina, strength and power in his or her professional or business life. If the left jaw is larger, strength was developed in the person's personal life.

Big jaws (jaws show when seen from back of head)

- **Committed to ideals**
- **Loyal**
- **Desires to dominate**

You have physical stamina and seldom surrender regardless of the odds. You can be truly committed and loyal to your ideals and principles. You have pride and integrity, and when you give your word you honor it. Your challenge is you may desire to dominate others.

Narrow jaws (face appears thin at jaws)

- **Not aggressive**

You avoid physical conflict. You are less aggressive and combative than someone with wide jaws and will seek mutually acceptable solutions through compromise. You have no desire to dominate or control others, and you resent and will resist others trying to dominate you. Your challenge is you may give up too easily.

Jowls (pads of flesh hang from jawline)

- **Commands respect**
- **Symbols of authority**

If you have jowls, you don't need a face lift. Jowls are symbols of authority that command respect. They indicate you have developed a sense of your own personal power and an ability to exercise it. In response to your jowls, others will tend to respect you and your opinions. You often see jowls on the faces of presidents and CEO's of large corporations. If the skin hangs loose or limp, it may indicate a loss of personal power or physical energy.

Ripples in jaw (ripples or pumping in jaw muscles)

- **Repressed anger**

You are experiencing tension and are repressing stored up anger, possibly even rage. While you may not be aware of these suppressed feelings, they are having a negative effect on your health and happiness. You may appear to be in control externally, but you are like a volcano that may erupt.

We have all been told at one time or another to "keep your chin up." Chins indicate our ability to keep going when times get tough and to rebound from a trauma or a shock. Chins also indicate how well we can take criticism.

Strong and well-defined (large chin)

- **Assertive and competitive**
- **Great perseverance**

You can be assertive, competitive, and aggressive. You have great perseverance. You possess a survivor's instinct and won't run from a fight.

Sticks out (chin protrudes)

- **Formidable adversary**
- **Not easily intimidated**

You will usually get the last word in any discussion or argument. You are a formidable adversary that never says "quit." You cannot be easily intimidated or bluffed.

Broad chin

- **Great physical endurance**

You have great physical endurance and can bounce back from setbacks and keep going. Your feelings are not as easily hurt as a person with a small chin. A chin like this is often found on managers and directors of large corporations.

Chins

Very broad chin (very wide)

- **Incredible resilience**
- **Physically demonstrative**

You possess an incredible resilience and are capable of rebounding cheerfully from a loss that would devastate most people. You are physically demonstrative and sex is an important form of communication for you.

Long chin (from mouth to bottom of chin)

- **Well grounded**
- **Innate physical power**

You have the same innate power as the person with a broad chin, and you are in touch with physical reality. You are well-grounded, but you may need to consider your thoughts more before you announce them to the world.

Small chin (delicate chin)

- **Sensitive to criticism**
- **Non-competitive**

You are sensitive and can be easily wounded by criticism. You don't need outside criticism, because you are already hard on yourself. You need encouragement and support from others. You are not aggressive and have little interest in competition.

Receding chin (mouth protrudes more than chin)

- **Avoids conflict**
- **High ethical standards**

You avoid conflict, seldom challenging others directly. You prefer consensus and agreement over assertive or aggressive behavior. You have high ethical standards and you expect everyone to follow the same rules you do.

Round chin

- **Compassionate**
- **Concern for people**

You have compassion, sympathy, generosity, and hospitality toward others. You have an interest and concern for people. You are kind-hearted, and when it gets down to acting on something, you put people first.

Straight chin

- **Motivated by causes and ideas**
- **Idealistic**

In your actions, you go all out for your ideas. You are high-minded and motivated by the causes that you believe in. Your focus is on getting the job done.

Chins

Pointed chin

- **Focuses on ideas**
- **Needs to stay in control**
- **Resists orders**

You are focused on ideas and staying in control. You have an ability to get your own way. The accomplishment of your goals is what is important. However, you are resistive to anyone giving you orders. You need an explanation first.

Very pointed chin (especially if long and protruding)

- **Can be domineering**
- **Puts goals first**

You can be very domineering in your desire to have your own way. You can be a tough customer in almost any situation and can be ruthless and efficient in accomplishing your goals. You put the accomplishment of your goals before the feelings of others.

Chin/Eyebrow Combinations

Understanding the relationship between the parts of the face is an important aspect of reading faces. We think and talk in terms of our upper face, but we act in terms of our lower face. So eyebrows indicate how we think or talk, while chins tell how we act on those thoughts.

Round chin/curved eyebrows

- **People person**

Your curved eyebrows indicate that your mental focus is on people, and your round chin shows a strong desire to help others. You have a warm and friendly nature. Sympathetic, generous and compassionate, you are a true people person.

Round chin/straight eyebrows

- **Pragmatic humanitarian**

Your straight eyebrows show your mental focus is on ideas and ideals, but your round chin indicates that you don't lose sight of people's needs and feelings. You are a pragmatic humanitarian.

Round chin/angled eyebrows

- **Self-appointed, responsible helper**

Your angled eyebrows show that you like to be in control, but your round chin indicates it's not because you want power over others, but rather because you believe that "if you want it done right, you better do it yourself." You seek harmonious results.

Chin/Eyebrow Combinations

Straight chin/curved eyebrows

- **Uses understand- ing of people to accomplish goals**

Your curved eyebrows show that you care about personal relationships, but when you shift into action, you will go all out for the causes or ideas that you believe will fix the problem.

Straight chin/straight eyebrows

- **Focuses on goals**
- **Extremely logical**

Accomplishing your goals in a logical manner is your focus in both thought and action. In your no-nonsense, logical approach, you can identify with Mr. Spock of Star Trek.

Straight chin/angled eyebrows

- **Military commander**
- **Mental control**
- **Focuses on objectives**

Your angled eyebrows show that you can evaluate carefully to form a plan then go forcefully forward, often intimidating others, to carry out your ideas. You would make a good military commander or chairman of the board.

Chin/Eyebrow Combinations

Pointed chin/curved eyebrows

- **Mover and shaker**
- **Promoter or political advisor**

Your curved eyebrows show a deep understanding of people, while your pointed chin indicates that you can use that understanding to shape and control the surrounding events. You are a mover and a shaker. You would do well as a promoter or as a political advisor.

Pointed chin/straight eyebrows

- **Focuses on accomplishing goals**
- **Less concerned about feelings**

Your straight eyebrows and pointed chin indicate that you are more focused on your causes and ideas than on people. You may take charge and carry out bold actions in accomplishing your goals, believing that the cause is more important than any individual. You are not afraid to break a few eggs to make an omelet.

Pointed chin/angled eyebrows

- **Detached**
- **Lacks compassion**
- **Will not compromise**

You are detached from people's feelings and can be very intimidating. If there are no softening qualities, like dimples, concave nose, abundant eyelids or full lips, you can be merciless and have no pity or compassion in carrying out your plans. You do not accept compromise of your ideals or goals and can skillfully manipulate a situation to achieve your aims.

"Wrinkles should merely indicate where smiles have been."

— Mark Twain , b. 1835 - 1910

American humorous writer.

"Circumstances alter faces."

— Carolyn Wells

American humorous writer.

"There's so much to say but your eyes keep interrupting me."

—Christopher Morley, b. 1890

American novelist, editor and man of letters.

SECTION II — FACIAL MARKS

One glance at the family picture album will quickly verify that we inherit some of our facial features. Some family resemblances persist for generations. Other aspects of our face our uniquely our own and are shaped by our own individual life experiences. Our face, just like our personality, is shaped by this combination of both "nature" and "nurture."

This is especially true of the lines on our face. No line on a face appears by accident. With its own metaphorical meaning, every line is a reflection of some habitual pattern of personal thought or feeling. These lines can be read as historical markers of the major events that shaped our lives. The degree to which our physical, mental, emotional, and spiritual components affect each other is truly amazing. The following incident illustrates just how interconnected we are.

I gave a presentation in which I explained that a person who has suffered a tragic personal loss will often develop a line that runs from the left corner of the mouth to the chin. I further stated that if the trauma was severe enough, the line could appear almost overnight. I mentioned the loss of a loved one or the loss of one's child as an example of such a trauma.

At the break, I was approached by two women, one of whom noted that she found my presentation interesting, but one part didn't apply in her case. She qualified her opinion by stating, "I don't know if it's because I have had two face lifts or because it was such a long time ago, but I lost a child twenty-six years ago and I don't have a line from the corner of my mouth to my chin." Before I could respond, her friend exclaimed, "You do have that line. It's right there," and lightly touched it.

The woman pulled out her pocket mirror and was dumbfounded. "I could have sworn I didn't have a line there!"

What she didn't realize was that when she recalled that painful memory, the grief line reappeared as she reconnected with the painful emotions associated with the death of her child.

I have seen this phenomenon repeated time and again. I have watched the courage lines on people's cheeks deepen as they shared the experience of facing their worst fears. I have also witnessed the indents or "secrets lines" at the corners of a person's mouth pull in at the very moment he or she emotionally withdrew. Every line reflects its owner's thoughts and feelings. By carefully observing the changes in the facial lines as the person speaks, you can develop deeper insights into what is transpiring within.

The following section delineates the meanings behind most of the lines you will see on people's faces. Lines are among the easiest aspects of face reading. Learn these and you will gain a far greater appreciation and in-depth understanding of each person you meet.

Dimples and Clefts

For beginning face readers, I recommend they start with dimples, clefts and lines. With other features, you must make comparisons. It can be difficult at first to determine what is a short nose versus a long nose, or high eyebrows versus low eyebrows. Accurately reading features comes with practice and careful observation. However, with dimples, clefts and lines, if you can see it, you can read it. It is that simple.

Dimples and clefts are softening features that indicate more playfulness, humor, and concern for others.

Good sport dimple (dimple in chin)

- Playful
- Good sport

You have a playful, good-natured approach to life and are a good sport.

Adaptability cleft (cleft in chin)

- Adventurous
- Extremely adaptable

You have an extreme playfulness and are adventurous. You are also extremely adaptable and may try many different jobs or relationships if the ones you have are not to your liking.

Destiny dimple (dimple in end of nose)

- May feel stuck in a job
- May have challenge with money

Your job needs to feel right to you. If it doesn't, you may find yourself questioning, "Is this my destiny; is this what I'm supposed to be doing?" Don't be afraid to follow your heart, even if others think you're flaky.

You may also have a challenge with money. At times, you can put yourself on a tight budget, but then "blow it" when you suddenly see something you can't resist.

Romantic dimple (dimple in one or both cheeks)

- Romantic playfulness

You have a romantic playful nature and love is important to you. Your focus is on matters of the heart.

Lines

Stop worrying about wrinkles and lines on your face! They are badges of honor for a life well-lived. Remember, if you can see the line, you can read it. The deeper and more noticeable a line, the more pronounced the quality it indicates. Deeper lines hold more meaning than fine lines. Don't forget that lines on the left side of the face are about personal issues. On the right side, the lines reflect issues in the external or outer life including career issues.

Mental development lines (horizontal lines on forehead)

- **Developed mental abilities**
- **Possible brilliance**

If you have three or more lines that run across your forehead, you have worked very hard at developing your natural mental abilities. The deeper and longer the lines, the greater the development. These could also be called genius lines, because when they run all the way across the forehead, they indicate brilliance in your field. If you have many broken lines, it indicates you have developed several mental interests.

Mental pressure lines (diagonal lines on forehead)

- **Mental concentration**

This indicates that through intense effort, you have developed your power of mental concentration in some specific areas. Their development resulted from an imposed mental discipline.

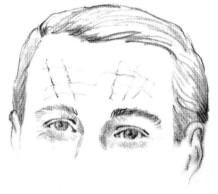

Freight train line (single deep line between eyebrows)

- **Self discipline**
- **Lets nothing stand in the way**

This indicates that you have developed a single-minded power of self-discipline and possible self-sacrifice. You let nothing stand in your way. Once you set a goal and get rolling, you are hard to stop! Your laser-beam focus is on details and being right. You need to be more gentle with yourself.

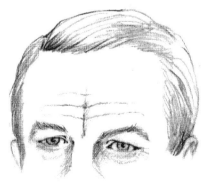

Lines

Forced focus lines (two lines between eyebrows)

- **Too hard on self**
- **Focuses on being exact and right**

This indicates that you have imposed a focused mental discipline in both your personal life and work life. You are too hard on yourself, demanding more of yourself than you ever would of someone else. Whether you feel like it or not, you take yourself by the collar and force yourself to get the job done.

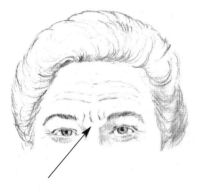

Perfectionist lines (many lines between eyebrows)

- **Perfectionist**
- **Wants everything in its place**

If you have more than two vertical lines between your eyebrows, you have perfectionist tendencies. You believe in a place for everything and everything in its place. You need to ease up and enjoy life a little more; don't make it so hard. You may want to ask yourself, "Why do I need to be so perfect?"

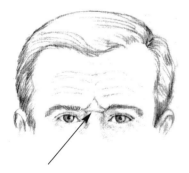

Visionary lines (triangle between eyes)

- **Inner wisdom**

This indicates that you have a strong connection between the left and right sides of your brain, giving you a dual perspective that allows you to access your internal vision and inner wisdom. You logically reason what is right and feel that it is so. You have an immediate capacity to see the deeper meaning beneath the surface.

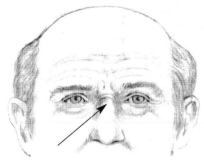

Responsibility lines (many fine lines on bridge of nose)

- **Very responsible**

You are overly responsible and assign yourself the difficult tasks. As a child, you may have been told that good people are responsible, and as a result you may take on too much responsibility.

Burn-out line (horizontal line on bridge of nose)

- **Overly responsible**

You have been so overly responsible that you have forced yourself to continue even when a task gave you no emotional satisfaction or mental stimulation. This "burn-out" line indicates you have now reached a stage where you need to find something to bring more joy into your life, even if it's just a hobby.

"Big picture" lines (radiating from outside corners of eyes)

- **Sees the bigger picture**

You have worked hard to develop a broader perspective and see the bigger picture. You have a better understanding of the relationship between all things. Your focus is more expanded and less gullible than in your youth. You realize if something sounds too good to be true, it probably isn't true.

Courage lines (diagonal lines across cheek bones)

- **Badges of courage**

You have had to access your deepest internal resources to confront the difficult circumstances life dealt you. These lines are badges of courage. On the left side, they show courage in facing personal problems. On the right, they show courage in facing professional or external problems.

Humor lines (lines on sides of the nose)

- **Mischievous**
- **Impish glee**

You have an interactive, playful, and sometimes mischievous sense of humor. You like to tease for fun. In fact, there may be a bit of impish glee in your humor.

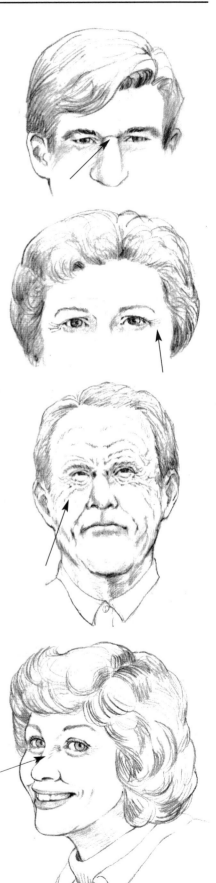

Lines

Disappointment lines (nose to corner of mouth)

- **Emotional disappointment**

You have experienced emotional disappointments. The deeper the lines, the greater the experience of disappointment. If the line is only on the left side, read it as inner world or personal disappointment; on the right, it is read as external world disappointments.

Compassion lines (corner of mouth to chin)

- **Deep emotional pain and loss**

You have weathered a traumatic emotional experience that may have included deep emotional pain and grief. On the left side, it indicates an intense loss or suffering, such as the loss of a loved one. If the line is on the right side, it may indicate severe loss in your external or business world. Because your heart has been opened by your own experiences, you have greater compassion for people and true empathy with their pain and suffering. The deeper the lines, the greater the sense of loss.

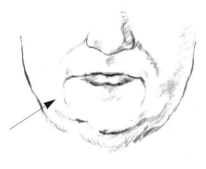

Forced smile line (horizontal line on upper lip)

- **Hides negative feelings**
- **Cut off from emotional support**

Your happy external appearance may not reflect your true internal feelings. You may often use a smile to hide your emotions. Your challenge is that you may not receive the nurturing and support you need and deserve from others because they may not be able to see past your smile.

Support lines (dimples that look like lines)

- **Lifts up others**
- **Gives encouragement**

You exert power by lifting up those around you and helping them feel better about themselves. In return they look up to and respect you. Because others expect your support and encouragement, your silence will often speak louder than words ever could in terms of calling attention to a problem.

Libido lines (vertical ridges under nose)

- **Divides world into male and female**

The more pronounced these lines, the more you may tend to divide the world into categories of male and female with specific roles for each. The wider apart these lines, the greater the sex drive in the individual and the greater the need for physical affection.

Survivor lines (vertical lines on upper lips)

- **Has overcome adversity**
- **A tested survivor**

These lines show the development of an inner personal strength born out of adversity. You have been hit by circumstances in life that felt totally overwhelming and perhaps even devastating. You may have faced what felt like a dark bottomless pit, and you had to dip into your deepest personal resources to pull yourself out to survive. You found a deep inner strength you didn't know you had. Today, you can face whatever life throws your way because you know you can handle it.

Gab lines (continuous line runs under chin and up cheeks)

- **Natural talker**
- **Communicates easily**

You have a wonderful, natural gift of gab and love to talk. In fact, you are a born talker and seldom run out of something to say. You never meet a stranger. This line shows strongest when you smile, which you do easily and often.

Desirability line (arch on chin)

- **Need to know you are desirable**

You may need confirmation of your sense of self-worth from external sources. You have a strong need to know that you are desirable from at least one person. A lack of childhood attention, appreciation, or just not feeling special may have given you a lower self-esteem than you deserve. Don't worry. People with a little lower self-esteem are easier to be around and more desirable than those with overblown egos.

Lines

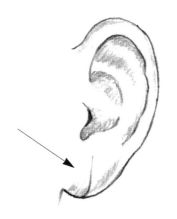

Heart lines (vertical line on ear lobe)

- **Heart problems**
- **Too hard on yourself**

Your focus in life is on doing and you may be too hard on yourself. If you push yourself too hard, it can lead to heart problems: just ask your doctor. Your challenge is to take better care of yourself. Pay attention to diet and exercise, get more rest, and find ways to put more joy, love, peace, and contentment into your life. Learn to measure your success by your ability to be authentic in every situation rather than judging yourself by outcomes and accomplishments.

Secrets lines (indents at corner of mouth)

- **Psychic trauma**
- **Closed on some topics**

There are some areas of your life that you do not choose to share and may never tell anyone. As a child, you may have learned that some topics were not safe, and you therefore prefer to hold them in rather than express your view or opinion. You have closed the door on some aspects of your life, feeling they are too painful or dangerous to deal with. To reclaim all of who you are, you may one day want to re-examine your reasons for closing off this part of yourself.

Obstinate chin (chin has a tense, bumpy appearance)

- **Steeled self to face world**

Because you don't expect life to be gentle or kind, you've hardened yourself to perpetually meet difficulties. You can be tough and even obstinate when challenged. You brace yourself for adversity and prepare to take it on the chin.

In face reading, everything counts, including facial hair. Just because someone has a mustache or beard covering part of his face doesn't mean you can't read it. In fact, it may give you more clues about the person's character than if he had no facial hair at all!

Mustache

- **Sensitive, but hides it**
- **Wants to appear very strong**

In face reading, upper lips express feminine energy. If you wear a mustache, you may feel self-conscious about expressing feminine energy. You hide your upper lip because you believe you will be ridiculed or that you won't be respected if others find out how sensitive you are. You want to appear strong at all times. You become defensive if your masculinity is questioned.

Beards cover up all the softening features on the lower face such as dimples, and indicate a desire to appear more masculine and authoritative. When reading beards, read the outside shape.

Round beard ("Santa Clause" beard)

- **Sensitive**
- **Concern for other people**

If you have a round beard, you may be covering up your softer side. You may be concerned that if people found out how softhearted you really are, they might take advantage of you, so you maintain a rough exterior. When you act on your ideas, you put people first and have a genuine concern for others.

Square beard ("Abe Lincoln" beard)

- **Focuses on ideas and ideals**
- **Assertive**

You feel a need to present a more forceful image in the pursuit of your ideas and ideals. You want to be taken seriously and have your authority respected.

Pointed beard ("Prince John" beard)

- **Goal-oriented**
- **Dominating presence**

Your focus is on accomplishing your goals. You let little stand in your way, including other people's feelings. When you act on your ideas, you are usually in control and often are a dominating presence.

SECTION III— FACIAL OVERVIEWS

We are all aware of poetic descriptions of faces. Everyone has heard of someone having "bedroom eyes," "kissable lips," "a rock jaw," or a "nose for business." These expressions are a familiar part of our language. Such overly subjective judgments, however, do not give us meaningful insights for classifying facial features. If we want to become proficient face readers, we must abandon our old methods for describing faces and develop a new vocabulary.

Face reading takes a more objective approach for evaluating faces by concentrating on the size, shape, position, and angle of various features. In addition to individual features, valuable information can be obtained from reading the face as a whole. The overall shape of the face can reveal another level of understanding that enhances our ability to form an immediate and accurate impression.

One interesting way to size up a face is by dividing it into three horizontal sections to determine which is the most prominent. The top section includes the forehead, from the hairline to the eyebrows. If this upper area is obviously the largest, you are dealing with a person whose focus is mental. Be sure to give them all the information and data available.

If the middle section, which includes the nose, is by far the largest, it identifies its owner as a person of ambition with a love of status and prestige. Any long-winded explanations won't work with them, so get to the point. However, a sincere and well-timed acknowledgement of their appreciation for quality will not be out of place.

Finally, if the bottom area, which includes the chin, is the largest, don't push! These people are earthy and well-grounded. They can't be stampeded into anything. Let them make up their minds at their own speed, and give them the space they need. They hate feeling crowded by anyone.

As you improve your skills, you will discover that the face contains its own self-diagnostic confirmations. The different parts of the face and their relationship to each other reveal the owner's life story. With practice, you move past seeing the pieces of the puzzle and begin to see each person's life history as a whole. The following section can give you additional information for developing that ability.

Face Shape

As you begin to really pay attention to faces, you will notice several distinct face shapes. While there are entire systems devoted to analyzing different face shapes, I have included those which are easiest to identify.

Broad or wide (wide or square face)

- Self confident
- Great strength and power

You possess natural self-confidence. In ancient face reading, your face would have been equated with that of a tiger with all its strength and power. You are not easily intimidated and don't fear a challenge.

Narrow or thin face (long or thin face)

- Feels fear
- Works best independently

Your initial approach may not be as bold as some others. You have had to learn self-confidence. You are proud of what you have learned and want an opportunity to apply what you know. Your challenge is fear, but remember that brave people are not those who never feel fear but rather those who feel fear and face it. You don't enjoy supervising others and prefer to work independently.

Diamond shaped face (wide at cheeks, narrow chin)

- Impatient
- Quick mind

This is a face that is both quick to anger and quick to love. You can be quite impatient. When you want something, you want it now! Your mind is fast and flexible, and you have no time for slow or stupid people. However, you don't want to be rushed when making up your own mind.

Pear-shaped (broadest under cheeks)

- **Peacemaker but not a pushover**

You are a peacemaker, but you may hide your own emotions in order to keep the peace. You put up emotional walls if others don't consult you, because you would always ask them. However, no one should underestimate you because you are no pushover. You have tremendous tenacity.

Flat-faced (no features protrude; face plane is largely flat)

- **Honest about feelings**
- **Polite and unassuming**

You avoid the limelight, are polite, and dislike attention. You are honest about your feelings. You do your job quietly, without making a fuss and without trying to get all the credit. You are helpful and want to share with others.

Face Types

In addition to face shapes, there is another way of looking at the face as a whole to determine some basic characteristics about the person. This is the face type. In typing faces, you have a combination of facial characteristics that tell about a general personality type. There are three basic types and mixtures of the three.

Mental type (thin face, large forehead, small jaw/chin)

- Intellectual
- Internal focus

Your focus is internal and intellectual. You are more connected to your inner thoughts and feelings than to the external world. Consequently, you may sometimes get lost or have trouble remembering people's names, even when you have just been introduced. You take refuge in your mind, retreating inward when troubled to figure out problems for yourself.

Physical type (large square face, big jaws and chin)

- Doer
- Needs space and freedom
- Competitive

You are a doer and respond to life with action. Possessing a competitive spirit, you love a challenge and physical activities. You approach life with a "can do" attitude and when troubled, will probably want to *do* something immediately. You need your freedom and personal space.

You also have a keen sense of geographical direction. Your challenge is in connecting with and expressing your feelings.

Emotional type (round face and chin, full cheeks)

- People person
- Likes good food
- Enjoys group activities

You are a people person and you connect easily with others. Physical comfort is important to you. You love celebrations, enjoy good food and like sharing it with others. You are probably one of those people who wants every celebration to be better than the last. You love to plan and direct group activities, including the making (or raising) and handling of money.

Combination Face Types

Mental/physical (broad forehead, square chin)

- **Mechanical ability**
- **Plans projects**
- **Active doer**

You like to do mental work in connection with some form of physical or mechanical activity. Your type is frequently found among promoters, engineers, inventors, architects, athletic managers, and the military's top brass. Your challenge is to connect with other people's feelings.

Mental/emotional (high, broad forehead, round chin)

- **Capable director**
- **Good manager**
- **Reserved about self**

You enjoy people and planning, but with a decided intellectual approach to it. You are probably inclined toward banking, politics, and finance and are quite perceptive about people. You connect with people's feelings, but may be inclined to keep your own to yourself.

Physical/emotional (square face, round chin)

- **Energetic personality**
- **Loves people and comfort**
- **Good sense of direction**

You have a strong people orientation and excel at planning group activities. You enjoy being physically active in whatever is going on. You combine a strong physical drive with a good mechanical ability, a love of physical comfort, and a good sense of direction. Your challenge is a fear of old age.

Facial Dominance

As discussed in the introduction to Part III, the face can be divided into three areas horizontally. When one is larger than the other two, it indicates an emphasis on the traits associated with that part of the face. It is also important to note when one area is much smaller than the other two. This usually takes some practice to see readily. As you study many faces, it will become obvious. If the areas appear to be nearly equal, dominance is not important to the reading.

Large upper area (from original hairline to eyebrows — not a receding hairline)

- **Focuses on ideas and information**
- **Loves distinctions**

Your focus is on thinking. You enjoy the world of ideas, and want to acquire knowledge, especially in your areas of interest. You like complete explanations with all the details. You love distinctions: how one thing is different from another. You prefer to judge the data yourself, and you want all the facts.

Large middle area (from eyebrows to nose tip)

- **Ambitious**
- **Appreciates quality**

Your focus is on status, luxury, and quality. You may also be ambitious, shifting into action to carry out your goals and dreams, but your secret desire is to be envied by everyone for your success. You enjoy the status of having the best. When others talk to you, you want them to get to the point. In selling to you, you need to be shown how an item is better than what you already have or how it will improve your status or success quotient.

Large lower area (nose tip to bottom of chin)

- **Wants practical applications of ideas**
- **Well-grounded**

You are well-grounded and like to see a practical application of ideas. Physically tough, solid and earthy, you have a good sense of yourself and your physical surroundings. You need time to make up your mind and refuse to be rushed. When you have a problem or need to make a decision, you think best when you can walk around or do something physical.

You may not be the first to speak up in a group, but when you do, others listen because you project integrity and sincerity.

Small upper area (forehead is the smallest area)

- Persistent
- Determined

You can be very determined, persistent, and intense. Not easily deterred, once you decide on a goal, you will let nothing stand in the way of your obtaining it.

Small middle area (nose area is smallest)

- Hard worker
- Well-respected

You are a hard worker and you always give 110%. Your challenge is in receiving the financial reward you deserve for your efforts. While you may not get rich, you will always be well-respected. It doesn't mean you can't gain wealth, just that you will work harder for it than someone with a larger middle area.

Small lower area (chin area is smallest)

- Sensitive
- Not physically grounded

You are a person of the mind and more connected to your inner world than your outer world. Extremely sensitive, criticism can wound you. You may not enjoy physical exercise and will do it only when necessary for some specific purpose or in connection with some other activity. Your challenge is with the physical plane. You may occasionally lose your sense of direction or forget people's names even after you have just met them.

Profile Types

Profile types combine facial features in particular groupings that form a gestalt that denotes a recognizable personality type. The convex profile includes a sloping forehead, large nose with a high bridge, a mouth that protrudes further than the chin and teeth that protrude outward. The eyes are full and quite prominent.

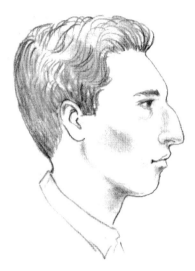

Convex (forehead angles back, nose most forward)

- **Quick mind**
- **Impulsive and impatient**
- **Directs others**

Your gift is a quick mind with an appreciation for systems and procedures and a practical approach in your thinking. While you may be quick in speech and action, your challenge is that you can be somewhat impulsive and impatient in your desire for tangible results. You prefer to direct others.

Extreme convex (prominent nose, extreme angle to forehead and chin)

- **Observant and energetic**
- **Fluent speech**
- **Quick in action**

Observant and energetic, you need only to see most tasks performed once to be able to do them yourself. Quick of mind and fluent in speech, you mentally outpace most people you meet. Your challenge is to overcome a tendency to be too aggressive or harsh, which may keep you from obtaining the full cooperation you need from others.

Moderately convex (mild angle to forehead and chin)

- **Tangible results**
- **More self restraint**
- **Gets cooperation from others**

Like the other convex types, you also focus on obtaining tangible results and appreciate efficient systems and procedures. You are more successful in directing others, because you have more self-restraint and a milder manner than the more convex face types.

Concave

The concave profile has a full round forehead which protrudes at the hairline, eyes are deep-set, the nose bridge is shallow and the nose is concave. The chin protrudes further than the lips with the teeth either vertical or sloping inward.

Concave (full forehead, protruding chin)

- **Creative problem solving**
- **Moderate energy level**

You are always looking for a creative solution to problems, and may seem easygoing with your meditative approach and moderate energy level, but you have a patient determination and can even be stubborn when confronted. Your challenge is being overly cautious and not taking enough risks.

Extreme concave (dish-shaped profile)

- **Mild-mannered**
- **Dreamer**
- **Procrastinates**

People may call you a dreamer and at times you may be absent-minded, but you have a sweet, mild-mannered, non-aggressive nature and are diplomatic in speech. Your challenge is a tendency to procrastinate.

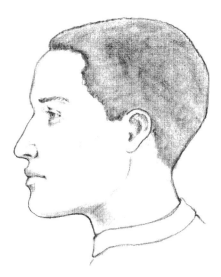

Balanced (neither convex nor concave profile)

- **Balanced thought**
- **Careful in speech**
- **Versatile**

You show a good balance between physical, mental and emotional areas of your life as well as between quick practical thought and slow, meditative thought. You are probably quite versatile and able to apply yourself in many directions. With so many possibilities open to you, your challenge is in deciding what you are going to do.

Profile Combinations

Combinations of convex and concave show characteristics of both types. The upper face is about thought processes, while the lower face is about implementing the thought into action.

Convex/concave (forehead slants back, chin protrudes)

- **Mentally quick, patient in action**
- **Thinks before speaking**

You have a quickness and practicality of thought along with a gift for memorization. You can be mentally aggressive but tend to be more diplomatic in speech and patient in action. You can pack a lot of substance into a few words. Your challenge is in speaking up before the moment to speak passes.

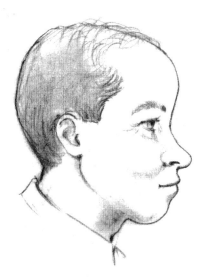

Concave/convex (forehead full, chin recedes)

- **Emotional approach to work**
- **May act without thinking**

You have an emotional approach to work and appreciate recognition for your efforts. Once you learn a task you can be quick in performance. Your challenge is to remember to think before you act.

The shape of the head can give you an instant gestalt on certain personalities. The following four head types have strong characteristics that you will see repeated in the features and/or lines on the face. The distinctive head shape provides an overall perspective which allows you to identify these characteristics even at a distance.

High crown/low forehead (highest point at crown)

- **Dominating**
- **Skeptical**
- **Persistent**

You have a quick, skeptical mind and insist on being shown. You demand facts as the basis of your judgments and care little for religion. You can be determined, persistent, hard to influence, and difficult to coerce. You may try to dominate others in your eagerness to have your own way. Your challenge is to develop sympathy, benevolence, and altruism toward others as you pursue your quest for power.

High forehead/low crown (highest point at hair line)

- **Hopeful, optimistic and trusting**
- **Discouraged by adversity**

You are an optimistic, hopeful person with a willingness to believe in others. You are trusting, sympathetic, and benevolent. Your challenge is with persistence and determination. You usually begin projects with high hopes; just don't allow yourself to become discouraged and give up before you are really defeated.

Head Types

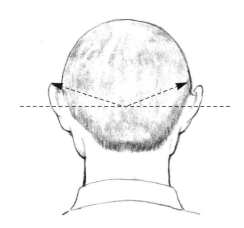

Round head (widest part is just above ears)

- **Fearless**
- **Dominating force**

You are fearless and plunge ahead, often throwing caution and prudence to the wind. You can be a very dominating force. Your challenge is to avoid becoming too reckless, impulsive, or shortsighted in your desire to rule.

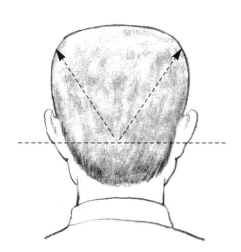

Square head (vertical rise above ears with flattened top)

- **Cautious and prudent**
- **Dependable**

You take a cautious, prudent approach. You are dependable and have moderate appetites and passions. Your challenge is that you are not a crusader, and you may be reluctant to go to battle for your ideals.

SECTION IV — APPLICATIONS

Many disciplines besides face reading give insight into personality. For example, psychological tests, enneagrams, neurolinguistic programming, handwriting analysis, astrology, numerology, and palmistry all produce some type of personality profile. However, face reading differs from other studies in one outstanding respect: the results do not depend on outside data from the subject. This helps eliminate inaccuracy in the profile caused by the subject, including problems caused by an uncooperative subject. In face reading, the subject does not have to take a test, answer questions honestly, produce a handwriting sample, provide a correct name, birth date, place of birth, or hold out a hand. If they have a face, you can read it.

The ability to make a quick and accurate personality inventory of people that does not depend on their mental or physical aptitude, honesty, or cooperation is an invaluable tool. It has applications in every walk of life, including sales, management, team building, relationships, and even jury selections. In fact, face reading is an asset in anything that involves direct interaction or communication with other people.

An additional bonus that face reading offers over other pursuits of personal insight is immediacy. While other disciplines require us to stop what we are doing to learn a system before we can apply it, we can study face reading with every personal encounter. By learning to read one feature at a time, we can build upon our abilities until we can see and comprehend every face as a map of the person's life. In fact, after learning to read faces, the phrase, "Don't I know you?" takes on an entirely new meaning.

In this section, a Features Summary gives you a quick reference guide to each feature. You may want to refer to it as we take you through two specific applications for face reading: sales and jury selection. This provides a take-off point for using face reading in other areas. After understanding what to look for in a given application, it's simple to apply elsewhere.

Features Summary

The face is a living map and there are no unimportant parts of it. Each feature reveals something. The following summary is a quick reference of keywords for the significance of each feature or area.

Forehead:
- Thinking style
- Mental development

Eyebrows:
- Mental processes
- Thinking patterns
- Mental approach

Eyes:
- Outlook on life
- Openness to others
- Emotional receptiveness
- Stress level
- Deception

Eye lids:
- Intimacy level
- Degree of openness or lack of openness

Eye puffs:
- Sensitivity to environment
- Discomfort

Nose:
- Work style
- Money matters
- Job requirements
- Trust issues

Nostrils:
- Generosity and expansiveness
- Energy level

Ears:
- Interaction with others
- Independence quotient
- Basis of reality
- Reception of data

Mouth:
- Self-expression
- Pessimism quotient

Lips:
- Manifestation of thoughts
- Sensuality/sexuality
- Emotional expressiveness

Teeth:
- Stubbornness
- Gumption
- Shyness

Smiles:
- Generosity
- Coyness
- Sincerity

Jaws:
- Personal strength
- Stamina
- Loyalty

Cheeks:
- Personal power
- Energy style
- Healing power

Chin:
- Assertiveness
- Aggressiveness
- Sensitivity to criticism

Dimples:
- Playfulness
- Humor
- Helpfulness

Lines:
- Gifts
- Challenges met

Facial hair:
- Hides sensitivity
- Read beards like chins

Ear/eyebrow combinations:
- Relationship between intake analysis and processing of information

Chin/eyebrow combinations:
- Relationship between mental perspective and final action

Face shape:
- Self-confidence
- Impatience
- Peacemaker

Face types:
- Mental
- Physical
- Emotional

Profiles:
- Personality gestalt

Head types:
- Domineering
- Cautious

Dominance:
- General life focus

Improving Odds in Sales

In using face reading in your personal and professional life, pay close attention to each person's face in any interaction. When you make a presentation to a group or walk into a board of directors' meeting, use the ideas below to help read your audience.

Who's got the power?

- Direct your attention to the person with the most promi - nent cheeks to speak to the person with the most personal power. If you convince that person, others may follow.

- To speak to the person who will probably get in the last word, direct your attention to the person with the largest chin or whose chin juts out the most.

- To address the person who is in control of the money, direct your attention to whoever has the longest nose or whose nose sticks out the most. A big bulb on the end of the nose means a person is very concerned about money.

- If there is a person with big jaws or jowls, pay attention. These are people who are used to getting their way. Use a respectful approach and be willing to listen, even if they interrupt you before you finish.

Facial dominance

If you can easily determine a person's facial dominance without having to guess, then use the following approaches.

Large upper area

- These are thinkers, so give all the technical information and details. Don't be afraid to use descriptive words or complex sentences. You have to win them over with logic and reason before you can finalize a sale. They love to see the differences and will check the warranty.

Large middle area

- Use verbs and adjectives and get to the point. Don't waste their time. Show them how they will be the envy of their neighbors or co-workers. Above all, give them results.

Large lower area

- Establish a connection first and don't press them to make immediate decisions. Let them make up their own mind in their own time. A more relaxed and easygoing approach works best with them.

Improving Odds in Sales

Eyebrows

Eyebrows indicate how a person thinks. The following approaches will help you establish rapport and get on their "wavelength."

Straight

- These are idea people, so use an approach based on ideas and facts.

Continuous

- These are powerful thinkers whose minds are always at work. Let them tell you some of their ideas.

Thin

- Especially if high, round and pencil thin, they need reassurance. Concerned with being judged, they want to be above reproach. In sales, a sincere compliment or two will help pave the way. Don't rush them. Remember, they may be self-conscious.

Tangled

- They will test your position by taking a devil's advocate stance. Don't start waffling when they challenge you; just clearly explain your side and be prepared to give facts. Don't let them get you rattled. They just like to shake things up to test the validity of the information.

Curved

- These are people-oriented individuals, so give them anecdotes and personal endorsements. Show them how it works in the real world.

Angled

- Ask for their opinions and how you can assist them. Let them know that their opinions are important, and allow them to feel in control.

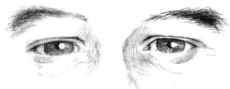

Managerial

- Use all the details and technicalities. You *must* know what you are talking about. They are mentally tidy and thrive on involvement in all the details.

Winged

- These people are visionaries. It's best to use some facts but cut out excessive detail. Show them the big picture and paint an enthusiastic vision of the possibilities.

Improving Odds in Sales

Face shape

Use the following approaches for these face shapes.

Protruding cheeks and big jaws
- Show respect for their opinions and viewpoints. They are accustomed to getting their own way.

Pear shaped
- Ask for their opinion again and again because they will put up emotional walls if not consulted.

Diamond
- If you want to make a sale with these people, you must get to the point (especially true if they also have high ears). They don't have time to waste and can be very impatient.

Flat
- These are polite people. Use a thorough presentation but nothing overly flashy or hyped.

Eyes

Eyes show a person's outlook.

Large eyes and/or small ears
- Make sure they are looking at you when you are talking. These people take in information best when they can see it, so use charts or draw pictures for them.

Straight bottom lids
- Basically mistrustful and suspicious, you must gain their trust before you can sell them anything. Once you do, they will be your most loyal supporters.

Eyes angle down
- These people look for the problems. Don't be too enthusiastic, and refrain from being jovial. To them, life is serious.

Eyes angle up
- These are optimists, so show them how great it will be. They expect everything to work out well.

Bulging eyes
- You may have a hard time trying to make your pitch because they won't stop talking. Be careful about interrupting because they may get their feelings hurt.

Recessed eyes
- These people just look like they are agreeing with you when they nod their heads. Actually, they are analyzing everything and need time to decide. Don't push them. Just give them more data until they make up their own minds.

Improving Odds in Sales

Nose

Use these approaches to appeal to different styles of logic.

Straight nose
- These people respect logic, so be sure your presentation is logical and clear. Avoid emotional appeals, and stick to the facts. Have answers.

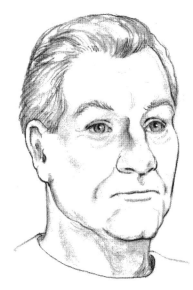

Bump on bridge of nose
- Don't make them feel cornered. State your position as strongly as you want, but stay open to them if they become feisty.

Concave (ski jump)
- These are people who respond to emotion, so show them how good they will feel or how good it will make someone else feel.

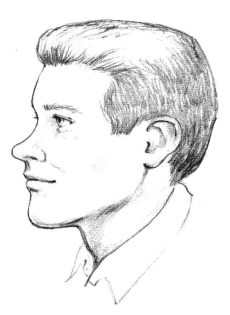

Arched
- These people appreciate beauty and creative new approaches. Be willing to listen to and appreciate their ideas and creative solutions. They like to have others implement their ideas.

Other features or lines to watch for:

The following details can make your professional life a lot easier by letting you know what to expect from a potential client. These little "flags" will clue you in to certain mind-sets and attitudes. Forewarned is forearmed.

Big gap in front teeth

- These people can be unpredictable, but they are willing to take a risk. Given a choice between staying with what they've got, or taking a chance on it all, they will often choose to go for it.

Crooked bottom teeth

- These are people who can see both sides and find it difficult to make up their minds. Reassuring them that they are making a good decision may be the most important feedback you can give them.

Mouth turns down

- These people are wary of what others tell them. It may be helpful to make a very balanced pitch by pointing out a few flaws or showing other alternatives to what you are selling. Your unexpected candor will help gain their trust.

Bigger upper lip

- It is important to be authentic. These people connect less to what you say and more to who you are. A slick presentation may sound phony and they are quick to spot deception. Relax and be yourself.

Improving Odds in Sales

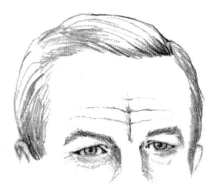

Freight train line

- If they get excited or start talking, they may be hard to stop. Don't worry, just wait patiently until they have finished and acknowledge their point of view before offering your position.

Reserved features

- These people have small mouths, thin lips, deep-set eyes and ears close to the head. They hold themselves in and are not outgoing. You cannot assume that you know what they are thinking or that they are agreeing when they nod their heads: that just means they heard what you said.

Additional selling signals

How can we tell when someone is open and receptive to what we are selling? Some additional signals that will tell us when a person is "buying" are included in the following checklist. Equally important are those subconscious early-warning signals that indicate that the person is rejecting what is being presented. For the purpose of clarity in the checklist, the buyer is the one receiving the information and the seller is the person presenting the information.

Positive signals

- **Buyer's bottom lids are rounded or curved.** This indicates a willingness to hear the information before passing judgment.

- **Buyer gestures with open palms** or palms displayed in the direction of the seller with fingers slightly cupped. This is a gesture of mental integration.

- **Buyer has a relaxed body posture** and relaxed facial expression. Remember, we tense our muscles when we feel threatened, frightened or defensive.

- **Buyer's gestures and facial expressions are congruent.** For example, the buyer nods his or her head yes when listening and responds positively, smiling and laughing at appropriate times.

- **Buyer's body movements are synchronous with seller.** Look for the buyer's pattern of gestures and body movement to mirror, match, or be in harmony with those of the seller.

- **Increase in the buyer's self-disclosure.** Notice when the buyer starts revealing more of his or her thoughts, and displaying a greater willingness to express feelings.

- **Buyer is willing to make direct eye contact** and appears open and enthusiastic.

- **Buyer rubs his or her chin.** While this might indicate that the buyer is feeling a little uncertain, it can also signal the buyer's subconscious acknowledgement of the seller's expertise or authority.

Negative signals

- **Beware of the smiling face with straight bottom lids** (the lower eyelids are straight across, covering part of the iris of the eye and the wrinkles below the eye seem to disappear). This can indicate an underlying wariness, guardedness or even anger that is not being expressed.

- **Watch for stiff-fingered palms and an extended, rigid thumb.** This is a control gesture warning people to remain at a distance. It also telegraphs, "I will not give up my position."

- **Also notice rigid or stiff body postures,** like arms folded tightly across the chest or tight, frozen facial expressions. When these are coupled with either little or no body movement, or sudden, erratic body movements, they are warning signs. The buyer is not relaxed and happy.

- **Additional negative signals include:** running or rubbing an index finger back and forth under the nose; rubbing the face; pulling the hair; or rubbing the back of the neck. (*The meaning of these gestures is detailed in Part V, Face and Body Talk, beginning on page 99.*)

- **Be aware of incongruent body signals,** such as shaking the head "no" when responding to a positive statement. Incongruent body signals often telegraph an internal conflict that isn't being expressed.

- **Indicators of strong sales resistance include** any or all of the following: buyer crosses their arms across their chest, crosses their legs and turns them away from the seller, turns their legs toward an exit, looks away, turns their back, or closes the door in your face.

Without a doubt, the greatest asset in sales is the ability to communicate. A successful sales person is often perceived as having a natural gift of gab. However, contrary to what we may think, the most important component of communication is not the ability to speak well, but rather the ability to listen well.

Becoming aware of the fact that every gesture, facial expression and body movement is an indication of an undisclosed thought or feeling will expand your communication skill beyond measure. When observing gestures and body movement as communication, remember that timing is of the essence. By becoming consciously aware of the context of the situation, you will discover hidden reactions. Ask yourself, "What happened or was being said when the gesture was made?" It will often give you a deeper insight into the person's unexpressed inner thoughts and feelings.

O ne of the most stressful times for many attorneys is the moment when the pre-trial motions have all been heard and the judge finally directs the bailiff to call in the jury panel.

In many instances, the lawyer may have worked weeks, months, or even years in preparation before the case comes to trial. However, in that moment, he or she is confronted with forty or fifty (and in some cases, over one hundred) strangers who know absolutely nothing about the case, and yet the entire outcome of the trial rests in their hands. They will decide who will win, who will lose, and what amount of money or punishment will be handed out, if any.

For most attorneys, the awesome responsibility of going through the process of selecting the final jury from the mass of people in the jury panel is at best confusing and at times, may seem hopeless. As any seasoned practitioner knows, often the least reliable information received is what comes out of the person's mouth. Nevertheless, voir dire is an attempt to sort out the jury panel by asking them questions and relying on their verbal responses, and when allowed by the court, relying on the information the potential jurors give in the juror questionnaires.

The problem with the voir dire process is that there is no way to know if potential jurors are being truthful, if they understand the questions, or if they are choosing not to cooperate with the system. Despite the lawyer's best efforts, the final selection of strikes may feel like guesswork. Just because a potential juror answered one question a certain way does not mean the answer, even if it was truthful, will be reflective of his or her final decision on the case.

The cognitive processes that form the basis for making any decision are so complex that it is almost impossible to predict a final outcome. The decision-making process is based on past experiences, values, thoughts, feelings, and even the events that occur in the heat of the moment at the time the decision is made. However, the purpose of jury selection is not to have a guarantee in predicting a juror's final decision. What is important is discovering if the potential juror has a predetermined mind-set, attitude or point of view that will make him or her an unacceptable jury candidate.

The best a lawyer can hope for in selecting a juror is to be able to determine general patterns. For example, is the candidate usually generous or stingy, open or guarded, trustworthy or deceitful, and is he or she going to base decisions on facts or feelings?

Every piece of information available to determine the candidate's character, values, attitudes, thought processes, and decision-making style is important. The person's dress, mannerisms, body language, gestures, and even what he or she is reading can give a perceptive observer insights into personality.

The focus here will be on physiognomy or face reading as a tool for developing insight into the personality style of the jury candidate. For a person skilled in the art, face reading gives a quick and reliable guide to the character and personality of the potential juror. It is extremely useful in jury selection where the ability to develop an accurate personality profile in the limited time given by the court can make the difference between winning or losing the case.

Each case must be evaluated on its own merits. It is important to look not only at the issues in your particular case, but also at the parties involved. For example, if you are representing an individual against a large corporation, it would be helpful to identify potential jurors who are typically focused on people issues and who can emotionally respond to your client. If you represent the corporation, you may prefer people who stick to the facts and don't let sentiment enter into their decision-making process.

If the issues in your case are important (for example, if your theory of recovery is based on fraud), you will want jurors who have high and rigid moral standards and who would find dishonesty especially offensive. If you represent the other side, you would prefer tolerant and easygoing types who believe anyone can make a mistake and are inclined to forgive them.

Another aspect of face reading may be even more important than the development of the juror profile. Face reading can give an accurate check of the individual panel member's responses during the voir dire questioning.

From experience, we know that we cannot always rely on what a potential juror says in response to a question. However, non-verbal responses, which cannot be easily controlled, can give an attorney important information about those panel members who have already made up their minds before hearing the first piece of evidence.

Juror profiles

While it may be impossible to predict with certainty a jury's final verdict, it is possible to improve the odds of a favorable outcome through better jury selection. Being able to develop an immediate and reliable personality and character profile of the individual juror can be invaluable. Having an insight into the way a person habitually responds or typically evaluates information can even help the attorney in the way the case is presented.

In each case, it is important to develop profiles of the best possible juror and worst possible juror based on the facts of the case and the parties involved. The following profiles are intended as aids to help evaluate potential jurors. It cannot be stressed enough that these profiles are not intended as final judgments on any potential juror, but rather as a guide to possible character traits that you might want a person on your jury to have. Face reading is not about black and white judgments. People are far too complex to try to attach some permanent label to them.

On the other hand, we are all face readers, and some of the most basic qualities and characteristics are clearly visible on every face if you know how to read it. The purpose of these profiles is to use them as guides to give you a vocabulary and structure for your perceptions and the other information you receive.

Damages

In cases where the principal issue is money, perhaps including questions of pain and suffering and/or punitive damages, the following is a partial face reading profile.

Plaintiff	Defendant
Generous people	**Financially conservative**
big lips	thin or no lips
broad nose	flat bottom eyelids
large round nostrils	small nostrils
People-oriented	**Fact-oriented**
round eyebrows	straight eyebrows
full cheeks	hard knobby chin
large ears	small ears
round chins	straight or pointed chins
Responds emotionally	**Mistrusts emotions**
ski slope nose	small iris
large iris	eye puffs over eyes
large upper eyelids	straight square chin
Identifies with pain	**High tolerance for pain**
thin face	broad square face
deep lines on upper lip	big powerful jaw
diagonal lines on cheeks	big protruding chin
Accepting/trusting	**Skeptical/mistrusting**
round bottom eyelids	flat bottom eyelids
up-turned mouth	down-turned mouth
full, loose lips	thin, tight lips
up-turned nose	nose tip turns down

The hung jury

In some cases where the other side has the burden of proof, a mistrial or hung jury can be almost as good as a verdict in your favor. A verdict requires that at least ten of the twelve jurors agree on the same points or issues. Therefore, it can be extremely helpful to spot people who seldom agree with others on anything.

Attracts conflict, devil's advocate
bushy, tangled eyebrows

Independent, non-conformist
ears stick out

Daredevil, risk taker
gap between front teeth

Has to be in control
pointed chin
protruding chin
angled eyebrows

Irritable, cantankerous, unpleasant
heavy, puffy upper lids
hard, knobby chin

Not interested in the opinions of others
very small, high ears

Motivated by self-interest
stretches upper lip across teeth when smiles
thin, or no lips
pointed chin
thin, pointed nose

Does not trust
flat bottom eyelids
down-turned nose
down-turned mouth

Freight-train personality
deep, single line between eyebrows
big powerful jaws

Suppressed anger, volcanic temper
jaw muscle pumping

Crazy and violent
white shows all around iris

Contracts

In suits where you are attempting to collect under a contract theory, you may want to look for conformists, business types, and people who trust institutions. Also look for people who are establishment-minded, self-confident, assertive, action-oriented, black-and-white thinkers who are slow to extend trust to others. In looking for these qualities, you may want to keep those who are:

Aggressive, competitive
  big, protruding chins
  square, muscular face
  big jaws
  high, prominent cheeks

Conformist, pessimist
  ears flat against head
  deep-set eyes
  eyes angle down

Wary, mistrusting, guarded and controlled
  angled eyebrows
  flat-bottom eyelids
  down-turned mouth

Not motivated by sympathy for others
  thin, arched nose
  nose tip hangs down
  thin or no lips
  small, high ears
  small nostrils

Decisions based on facts
  low, straight eyebrows
  straight, square chin
  long, straight nose
  sloped-back forehead

The foregoing profiles are intended as an aid to help evaluate potential jurors. *It cannot be stressed enough that these profiles are not intended as final judgments on any potential juror, but rather as a guide to possible character traits that you might want a person on your jury to have.*

"Don't laugh at a youth for his affectations; he's only trying on one face after another to find his own."

— *Logan Pearsall Smith, b. 1865 - 1946*

English essayist and critic.

"If you do big things they print your face, and if you do little things they only print your thumbs."

— *Arthur ("Bugs")Baer, b. 1897*

American comic and short-story writer.

"There are no broken faces. Your face reflects your personal survival strategy. The fact that you are here to read this book means your strategy is working."

— *Mac Fulfer*

Section V — Face and Body Talk

In previous chapters, we have studied the physical form of the face to develop insights into the person's habitual thought patterns, character traits, and emotional needs. We have seen a connection between our physical, mental, emotional, and spiritual aspects and that each aspect reflects the others.

However, there is another equally exciting aspect to face reading that can add a dimension to our understanding of people. This aspect focuses on our energy centers.

As humans, we are much more than a physical body. Each of us is animated by a life force and energy that flows through us, around us, and even between us. Scientists can measure the various electrical impulses that flow through us with EEG's, EKG's, MRI's and an enormous battery of diagnostic tests. Kirlian photography shows an energy field that surrounds us like an aura. Throughout the centuries certain people have been acknowledged for their healing touch, which has been developed in the art of reiki. And, on a personal level, most of us have at one time or another felt that unexplainable spark of energy called love that passes between us.

As we saw in earlier chapters, each part of our face has a structural significance as well as a metaphorical meaning. This is true of our entire body. Each part of our body has a corresponding energy center. These centers have been studied and mapped in some cultures and may be called chakras, meridians, pressure points, or vortexes depending on the discipline. We all possess these energy centers and we constantly energize them on an unconscious level.

If we look at ourselves as energy centers, one of the first things we notice is the importance of our hands. Our hands have more nerve endings than almost any other part of our body. In fact, our hands confirm our reality. Even as infants we pick up or touch objects to test their reality and then usually double-check ourselves by immediately trying to put them in our mouth. Our hands not only radiate warmth and soothing touch, they also give off energy. Consequently, noticing what a person does with his or her hands can be extremely revealing. Our hands energize and affect our energy centers.

For example, if you are talking with someone who suddenly puts his left hand in his pocket, what could that reveal? It could just mean that his hand was cold. Recalling that our left side is our personal side, it might also indicate that the person is hiding something in his relationships, emotional side, or personal life. By beginning to be consciously aware of the gestures others make in the course of a conversation, you can increase your personal awareness level.

The unconscious gestures we make with our arms and hands are not random acts. They reflect our personal patterns of thought and feeling, just as our face does. Be aware, however, that there can be many reasons for people to put their hands in their pockets or scratch their noses. It cannot be stressed enough that all gestures must be taken in context.

The following is a guide to understanding the unconscious gestures we see people make every day. Most of these are connected with our face, but I have also included some that illustrate the total interconnectedness throughout our body.

Hands are our most mobile energy center and energizer. They are also a metaphor for how we hold on, reach out, or withdraw from life. The gestures you see in hands are ongoing clues as to what is passing through a person's mind at any given moment, many times unconsciously. It is important to notice which hand is being used to make a gesture.

Hiding left hand

• **Hiding something personal**

If in a conversation a person hides his hand, it is important to notice which hand he hides. If he hides his left hand in his pocket, he consciously or unconsciously may not want to reveal something about his relationships, personal life or personal feelings. For clues, look at the context of the conversation or events surrounding this gesture.

Hiding right hand

• **Hiding something external**

If the subject suddenly hides his right hand, he may be guarding some aspect in his external or professional life. For example, if I asked the price of a used car and saw the salesman suddenly put his right hand in his pocket before answering, I would wonder what was not being said. Was there a problem that was being concealed?

Steepling (finger tips together or interlocked)

• **Wanting to appear in control**

In addition to fingertips together, there are several variations of this gesture. For example, you may see fingers interlocked with the index fingers raised in a steepling posture. This is a gesture often used by people in authority or who feel a need to be in control of a situation. You may see a supervisor lean back and put his or her fingertips together which indicates a need to appear more confident and secure than he or she is feeling at the moment. It is an outward sign of wanting to appear superior, in charge, or in control, but it also reflects that the person is not nearly as confident as they would like you to believe.

Gestures

Holding thumbs

- Anxiety
- Doubt or worry
- Feeling threatened

Our thumb is a metaphor for our head. Holding a thumb is a metaphor for trying to cover our head with our arms for protection. When you notice someone holding his thumb, it is a sign that he is feeling threatened. Babies hold their thumbs when in distress.

Holding the left thumb may indicate feeling threatened on an internal or personal level. The person may be feeling fearful, uncertain, uncomfortable or insecure at that moment. Holding the right thumb may indicate feeling threatened by something in the external environment. Holding both thumbs indicates a more extreme anxiety, emotional discomfort, doubt, worry, or fear.

Holding a thumb is often an unconscious gesture. If you catch yourself holding your thumb, bring it to your conscious awareness level and ask yourself, "What is causing me to feel threatened?" Check to see which thumb you are holding to discover clues to whether it is an internal fear or a perceived threat in your environment.

Stiff thumb and/or hand

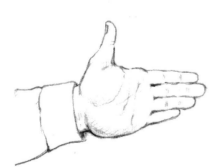

- Won't budge on position
- Wants to dominate

Another important thumb signal is the person who gestures with an extended, stiff thumb. This may include gestures with stiff and extended, straight fingers or a tight fist with the thumb extended. Whatever the variation, this gesture is indicative of a person who is firmly planted and will not budge on their position. They may want to dominate in the situation or at least be in charge and will stubbornly hang onto their point of view without compromise. If you are trying to sell this person on a contradictory point of view, you have your work cut out for you!

Scratching or rubbing top of head

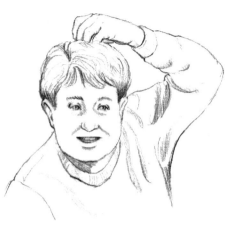

- **Confusion**

When the energy center at the top of the head is blocked, we will unconsciously scratch or rub the top of our head. This gesture indicates possible confusion. If a person scratches his head while you are explaining something, he may be communicating his confusion. Ask if he understands, give him an example, or repeat the information.

Rubbing the brow

- **Doubt or worry**

We hold worry and doubt in our forehead or brow. A person rubbing his brow can be unconsciously signaling a feeling of doubt or worry. If you find yourself rubbing your own forehead, stop to identify what is causing you to feel worried or doubtful. Often by consciously identifying the source of the concern, we can correct it.

Tapping or pressing between eyebrows

- **Forced recall**

Schoolchildren taking a test will sometimes tap the space between their eyebrows with the eraser end of their pencil when they are stumped on a question. This spot is sometimes called the third eye and is the area of self-will. Tapping this spot can indicate an effort through self-will to focus, concentrate, or recall the answer.

Variations you see among adults is pinching the bridge of the nose between the eyes or pressing a thumb to the spot between the eyebrows. These are also gestures of forced recall by attempting to focus the inner will and often indicates the person may be experiencing some sort of physical, mental, or emotional block at that moment. A headache can be such a block.

Gestures

Rubbing eyes

- **Mental exhaustion**
- **Feeling over-burdened**

Eyes may well be "the windows of the soul," but they are also where we store exhaustion, exasperation, and the anger we feel when we are over-burdened. The unspoken meaning behind eye-rubbing is, "I've had enough." If you find yourself rubbing your eyes, bring this non-verbal communication to conscious awareness and take a break. Often our bodies will communicate our limits more clearly than our minds.

Pinching, pulling, scratching or rubbing the nose

- **Feeling pressured or controlled**

There are several variations of this gesture including simply running a finger across the bottom of the nose. Of course, the person could be just wiping his nose, but it could also mean more.

Our nose is where we store the fear of being controlled by others. If you ask a friend, "Could you help me move this sofa?" and before he answers he rubs his nose, even if his answer is affirmative, he has first said with face talk that he is feeling pressured or cornered and would rather not.

Fingertips touching temple

- **Mental saturation point**

You may sometimes see a person who appears to be propping up his head by placing a thumb under the chin and index finger on the temple. This indicates an effort to pull assertive energy from the chin area and send it into the brain. What the person is saying is that he or she is fast approaching the mental saturation point.

Covering the mouth while listening

- **Critical evaluation**
- **Disbelief of what is being said**

This is a gesture I am very aware of in jury trials. If I see members of the jury panel covering their mouths during testimony, it is a metaphor for wanting to cover the mouth of the witness. It signals they don't believe what is being said.

When you see this gesture, at that moment the person is critically evaluating what is being said and generally disbelieves whatever he or she is hearing.

Covering the mouth while talking

- **Fear of speaking**
- **Hiding something**
- **Shyness**

The mouth is about expressing ourselves. Covering the mouth while speaking can have several meanings. The person could be shy and afraid to express him or herself. It could stem from nervousness, or trying to hide something or possibly a lack of truthfulness. Look at the context of the gesture for clues.

Holding the chin

- **Feeling insecure or inferior**

The chin is a personal symbol of aggressiveness, competitiveness, or power. A person holding his chin subconsciously wants a bigger chin or greater power. Since we store fear of inferiority in the chin, holding the chin indicates a person is unconsciously signaling uncertainty or a feeling of inferiority.

Gestures

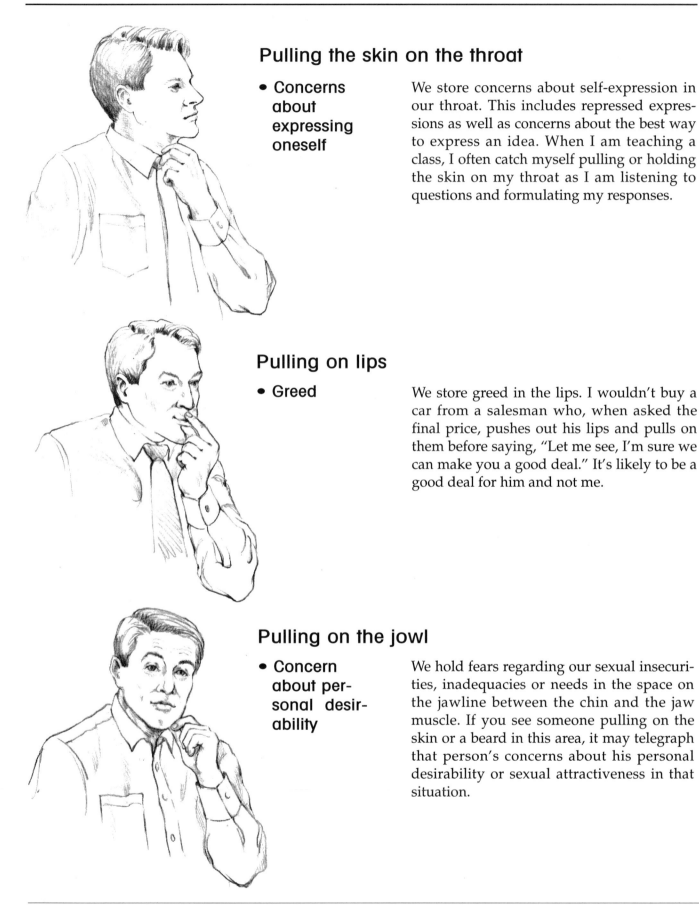

Pulling the skin on the throat

- Concerns about expressing oneself

We store concerns about self-expression in our throat. This includes repressed expressions as well as concerns about the best way to express an idea. When I am teaching a class, I often catch myself pulling or holding the skin on my throat as I am listening to questions and formulating my responses.

Pulling on lips

- Greed

We store greed in the lips. I wouldn't buy a car from a salesman who, when asked the final price, pushes out his lips and pulls on them before saying, "Let me see, I'm sure we can make you a good deal." It's likely to be a good deal for him and not me.

Pulling on the jowl

- Concern about personal desirability

We hold fears regarding our sexual insecurities, inadequacies or needs in the space on the jawline between the chin and the jaw muscle. If you see someone pulling on the skin or a beard in this area, it may telegraph that person's concerns about his personal desirability or sexual attractiveness in that situation.

Rubbing behind ears

- **Fear of not being understood**

We store fear of misunderstanding or being misunderstood behind the ears. If you are explaining something to someone and they start rubbing behind their ears, they are telling you "I don't think I got that, could you go over it again?" It would be a good idea to repeat yourself, or perhaps explain it in a different way.

Rubbing the back of the neck

- **Would rather not think about it right now**

In the back of our neck, we store repressed thoughts and things we would rather not think about or deal with at that moment. For example if a person rubs the back of his neck when asked, "Are you going to mow the yard?" he is saying in face talk, "I'd rather not think about that right now.

Cheeks tighten, blush or droop

- **Embarrassment**
- **Humiliation**

From an earlier chapter we learned that cheeks represent our personal power and pride. On an energetic level, our cheeks also hold shame and embarrassment. If someone is caught in an embarrassing incident, his or her cheeks may turn red. If the situation is even more humiliating, the cheeks may appear to sag or droop.

Gestures

Body

Arms folded across chest

- **Holding a position**
- **Self protection**

Energetically, our arms are symbols of how we embrace the world and in turn how we are embraced. Our arms are what we hold on with. Folding arms across the chest communicates that a person is holding his position (and from a pre-language perspective, protecting his vital organs). If a person folds his arms in front during a conversation, it might be wise for you to initially imitate this posture. It is almost making a statement that, "If you feel a need to guard yourself from me, then I will guard myself, too." After the tension leaves the air, you might try unfolding your arms to signal a truce or the invitation, "I will lay down my arms if you lay down yours."

Drooping shoulders

- **Too much responsibility**

We hold responsibility in our shoulders. Just like the mythical Atlas, we often find that we hold the weight of the world on our shoulders. Drooping shoulders may indicate a person who is carrying more responsibility than he or she desires.

Arms behind back

- **Fear of being touched**
- **Fear of reaching out**
- **Hiding something**

Arms behind the back may indicate a fear of reaching out to touch or connect with another person, or a fear of being touched. Of course, if the arms are behind the back, so are the hands, which may indicate a strong desire not to reveal anything.

Small of the back

- **Stress**

We hold stress in our back, especially in the small of the back. This stress includes physical, mental and emotional. If you find your back hurting, ask yourself what you were doing or thinking about that was stressful. Sometimes by identifying the cause, we can cure the symptom.

Buttocks

- **Fear of failure**

We hold fear of failure in our buttocks. It is no surprise that people who are seen as thwarting our goals, or creating problems for us are sometimes referred to as "a pain in the butt."

Thighs

- **Fear of lack of capacity**

We hold fear of lack of capacity in our thighs. When we push past our limits or take on too much, we often feel tension or an ache in our thighs. When this happens, ask yourself what you're feeling overwhelmed about.

Knees

- **Fear of death**

We hold fear of death behind our knees. If you ever encountered a reckless driver who caused you to take defensive action, even if you successfully avoided the accident, you may have found your knees were a little wobbly when you got out of the car.

Calves

- **Fear of lack of capability**

Fears about our lack of capability are held in our calves. Can I really do this? Am I able? When you feel tightness or stress in your calves, stop to consider, "Where am I questioning my capabilities?" Of course, you may just be spending too much time on your tiptoes! Remember, there can always be more than one explanation for bodily sensations.

Feet

- **Fear of being ourselves**

We hold fear of being ourselves in our feet. Since ancient times, people have known that massaging someone's feet is one of the best ways to draw them out and put them at ease. If someone is ticklish or won't let you touch their feet, it is a form of body armor. On some level, they may be fearful about you really seeing or knowing them. They are communicating a need for a boundary.

Summary

Using This Information

Once you learn where the body's energy centers are located and also understand what meanings they hold, you can begin using this information to enhance your overall reading. Notice what the person is doing with his or her hands. Remember, our hands are mobile energy centers that we unconsciously use to move or interact with energy in our body. Also listen for expressions of physical discomfort. You soon learn that everyone is giving out as many signals as a baseball coach signaling in plays.

Your awareness of gestures will soon shift from picking up isolated signals to receiving a whole string of information. You can even use this information to increase your own self-awareness. As stated before, our bodies often understand more about our present situation than our minds do.

As an example of how you might use this information if you find yourself feeling anxious or uncomfortable, you might try the following exercise:

Take a moment to sit or lie down and let your body relax. You may even want to use a relaxation technique like counting backwards from twenty. As you count to yourself, imagine you are walking down an incline, relaxing more and more with each descending number. After you are relaxed just ask your body, "What is troubling me?" Or maybe, "What is the truth about my present situation?" or "What is it that I could know that would help me now?" Then listen to your body by noticing all the various sensations you feel. For example, you might notice a tingle in your scalp, a tightness in the back of your neck, and a small ache in your buttocks.

Using the information you can decipher and translate these body signals. In this example, I would ask myself what am I feeling confused about and what don't I want to think about because I am afraid I might fail. With this information we can often suddenly see exactly what was creating our stress. "Oh yes, now I remember. The teacher gave us an assignment that I didn't quite understand and I've been trying not to think about it because I'm afraid I won't get it right anyway."

Developing Perception

Learning to apply the information gained from observing people closely is like stepping into a new world. The ability to see people from a new perspective and understand them on a deeper level has the potential to not only expand your perception, but to open doors you never knew existed.

As a word of caution, there are no absolutes in reading people. I always leave open the possibility that I could be mistaken. It has never been my experience that anyone reported that a reading was totally wrong, but I don't try to impose readings on people. It is perfectly permissible for a subject to disagree with an insight. In fact, some of the very best information I have received for developing my own understanding and clarity was from subjects who disagreed with some aspect of their reading.

Also realize that if the subject over-reacts or denies your insights, the reading may be accurate, but you may have accidently crossed a person's comfort boundary without their permission.

The best way to use the information in this chapter is to become aware of the possibility of deeper meaning in every action and gesture. I certainly acknowledge that there can be more than one reason for any given behavior. However, if you start to notice how many times your observations are accurate, you will begin to see the true value of learning to read people. Your own self-confidence and ability to communicate will dramatically increase as you develop a deeper understanding of every person you meet.

"The first thing I do in the morning is brush my teeth and sharpen my tongue."

— *Oscar Levant b. 1906*

American pianist, composer, and wit.

"Her features did not seem to know the value of teamwork."

— *George Ade, b. 1866 - 1944*

American humorous author and playwright.

"What a blessing it would be if we could open and shut our ears as easily as we do our eyes."

— *Georg Christoph Lichtenberg, b. 1742 - 1799*

German physicist satirist and miscellaneous writer.

Section VI — Sample Readings

In the first chapter, we began to look at faces differently, understanding that our face reflects our life history. We discovered that face reading is like learning a new language: the first task is to develop a meaningful vocabulary. Next, we learned to classify the parts of the face by learning to separate and identify the various features. Then, we begin to see how all the features relate to each other and how each line has a meaning. Finally, we begin to see the face not only as a complete story of the person's life, but also as a communication tool that is responding in the moment to the person's every thought and feeling.

Now it's time to pull it all together. In this section we begin to actually read faces. In the first two sample readings, you may want to test your skills by first looking at the illustration and reading what you can see before you read the explanation given. A good way to learn face reading is to identify the features and lines that you can observe and then look up their meaning. Compare your reading to the sample face reading profile.

To help you in your development as a face reader, the third sample reading in this section includes a face reading quiz, giving you an opportunity to test your ability to connect meanings with the features and lines on a face. To get the most out of this quiz, first study the illustration closely. Identify all the lines and features that you find and look up their meanings. Read the face reading analysis and compare your answers with those provided.

You can also check your ability to identify the features and lines by reading the answers to the quiz on page 122-123.

Sample Readings

W̲e have all heard that a picture is worth a thousand words. Face reading verifies the truth of that adage and adds a totally new dimension to the study of historical figures. For example, what can we tell about the mighty Indian warrior, Chief Sitting Bull from just his picture?

One of the the first things you notice are Sitting Bull's broad, prominent, and powerful cheeks. His cheeks identify him as a bold leader who could capture the attention and respect of others by his mere presence. They reflect enormous reserves of personal power. However, a closer look at his cheeks reveals that he was a man whose courage was truly tested. Those deeply etched courage lines show that his personality and character were forged by overcoming tremendous adversity and by facing what may have felt like impossible odds.

Just below his cheeks we see Sitting Bull's strong, bulging jaws which reflect an undaunted tenacity, personal integrity, and physical stamina. His jaws give him such a formidable presence that few would dare argue with his final decisions. Powerful jaws also predict that when he gave his word, he would keep it.

Leadership ability is also reflected in his large, arched nose which indicates an ability to take charge and a need to make a significant contribution in the final outcome. The Cupid's bow on his upper lip shows an ability to manifest whatever goal he set for himself. Even his chameleon eyebrows would give him an advantage in negotiations, allowing him to gain information from the other side while never telegraphing his true feelings or position on any topic. His thin lips verify that he played his cards close to his chest and never revealed anything until he was ready.

A strong, straight chin with rounded corners would indicate that he was a person who would go all out for the goals, ideals or causes he believed in while guarding the general welfare of those close to him. The tension in his chin shows he didn't expect

Sitting Bull (1834 - 1890)— Chief of the Hunkapappa Sioux

the world to be gentle, easy, or kind, but approached every day as a battle to to be waged. This attitude is reflected many times in the chief's face and shows the tremendous degree of internal consistency that we find in faces.

For example, the almost straight bottom lids indicate that he was wary, suspicious, and guarded, dividing the world into "us" and "them." He would need proof before he would give acceptance and even then would need to be shown. This lack of trust is also visible in his down-turned nose tip and down-turned mouth. He mistrusted what he was told by others and expected the worst. History verifies that he was probably justified in this attitude. The heavily marked lines from his nose to the corners of his mouth confirm that he was profoundly affected by the disappointments and broken promises, especially in his external life since the line is more deeply etched on the right side.

Looking further, we see that he was not just a leader, but also a concerned provider who put the needs of others first. His broad nose shows that he immediately extended a broad umbrella of support over those he bonded with and his enormous nostrils demonstrate that he was generous to a fault with those who relied on him even when he took on too much personally. In fact, the horizontal lines on the bridge of his nose mark him as being overly responsible and the vertical lines between his eyebrows show he was not just hard on himself, but demanded perfection.

Being a chief was no easy job, even for a man with his talents. The stress of too much external focus is evident in the mild puffs in his upper eyelids. The vertical lines on his upper lip bear witness to his ability to survive circumstances that would have destroyed a weaker person.

A surprise that face reading reveals about Sitting Bull is the fact that he would probably have been happier as a medicine man. His lack of jowls indicates that he took no delight in having power over others and his lack of visible eyelids reveals a great need not only for his own personal space, but solitude. Observe that his right eye looks directly and defiantly out into the world. However, on his personal side, his left eye is turned to look within at an internal realm. This dual perspective gave him the unique spiritual insight usually reserved for a shaman or mystic. The survivor lines on his upper lip reflect personal battles as he descended to his depths and passed through a dark night of the soul in search of his own private vision.

Finally, the way his cheeks protrude at the sides are the mark of a healer. He had a natural ability to lift up, nurture, and heal others and to share his knowledge. His wisdom is revealed in the horizontal lines on his forehead showing that he stretched his mind in more than one area and worked hard at developing several mental interests. Furthermore, the crow's feet at the corners of his eyes are testimony to the breadth of his vision: he could see the big picture even though he was unable to change it.

Sample Readings

In school we all learned that Benjamin Franklin was a man of many talents. He was an inventor, writer, printer, philosopher, statesman, scientist and diplomat. But what does his face say about who he really was?

First, his broad, high, round, and full forehead tells us he was a thinker. Not content with the tried and true methods, he was always looking for a new approach and a better idea. The lines on his forehead show that he developed a wide range of interests. He loved distinctions and was good with logic, theory, and academics. However, the length from the bottom of his nose to his chin shows that he was no mere academician, but had a keen awareness of physical reality and a need to bring his thoughts and ideas down to earth with some practical value.

His eyebrows give us insights into his complexity. In his personal life, his mental focus was people-oriented with a quickness that allowed him to see all the related aspects of a situation immediately. On his professional side, he has a managerial eyebrow. Once he accepted a task he would stick with it to the bitter end, making sure all the i's were dotted and the t's crossed. The scattered hairs at the end of the eyebrow also show a wide range of mental interests, confirming what we already saw in the lines on his forehead.

Ben had low ears and high eyebrows, proving he was a patient listener and a gifted strategist. He would take in all available information, give himself time to put the data on his mental framework, then develop a plan of action. His large ear lobes show he was especially observant and keenly aware of the appearance of things. The diplomatic slant of his ears reveals his skills at creating conciliation between opposing groups.

Broad, full cheeks set wide apart gave him not only the stamina for the long haul, but also the capacity to gain a consensus. He would have been seen as tolerant, non-judgmental, and accepting, so others would have felt comfortable joining him. His openness to ideas and to others is marked in the roundness of his bottom

Benjamin Franklin (1706 - 1790)— American Statesman, publisher, inventor, scientist, ambassador and writer.

eyelids, showing that he wanted to hear all the facts and didn't screen out important information. We can see from his picture on the U.S. one-hundred dollar bill that he was experiencing mental stress, especially in his personal life. Of course, the white showing between his iris and bottom eyelid could be about stress in his personal relationships and history tells us that was certainly a possibility. Or perhaps finding his face on a one-hundred dollar bill is stressful for the man who invented the phrase, "A penny saved is a penny earned!"

We can learn volumes from Ben's nose. The large size confirms a need to make a major contribution in life. Professionally, he would need to own his own business, or at least control the pace and style of work. The width shows that he would immediately shelter and defend those close to him. His large nostrils tell us he felt a sense of personal abundance and may have been overly generous. A well-known philanthropist, Ben established many institutions for the common good, including schools, hospitals, and libraries.

Don't get the idea that Ben was a pushover, however. The high bridge of his nose tells us that he was independent, self-reliant, and needed to be in charge of his work environment. He wouldn't tolerate someone standing over his shoulder, telling him what to do. Furthermore, that bump on the bridge of his nose says he could be feisty if backed into a corner. Finally, the tip of his nose is somewhere between a bulb and a small ball. He probably possessed both qualities; a concern for money that came from an impoverished childhood and a creative, artistic appreciation for beauty.

Ben was blessed with a powerful persuasive ability that is shown repeatedly in his face. First, he had the thin upper and full lower lip of a natural salesman and promoter. He could convince others of his position while keeping his innermost feelings hidden. The huge chin says that when he did speak, he often had the last word, again supported by the powerful jowls that communicate personal authority, and a freight train line between his eyebrows that tells us when he made up his mind, he let nothing stand in his way. When he spoke, others listened.

Yet, Franklin was no bully. His abundant eyelids gave him a charismatic ability to connect with others and make them feel that he would have compassion and tolerance for different points of view. One of his gifts would be an ability to bring people of different convictions together, which is borne out by history. He has been credited with keeping the Constitutional Congress of 1787 in session when it was about to disintegrate into petty quarreling.

This brings us to Ben's personal life. What was he like when he wasn't being a statesman, scientist or publisher?

His thin upper lip indicates that as a child, he was held to impossibly high or rigid standards and therefore didn't talk much about his feelings, or for that matter, his personal life. Nevertheless, his large upper eyelids confirm that in his personal life, he had a great need for intimacy. His life focus was on cultivating, building, and maintaining relationships. He wanted to share life and needed strong, intimate connections. The broad space between the vertical lines on his upper lip verify his powerful libido, and historically, we know that he was ridiculed for consorting with "low women." Yet, from his round chin, abundant eyelids, broad nose, and the downward slant of his left eye, we can see that the truth was he had a strong compassion and acceptance for everyone, including the poor and downtrodden.

Ben's life was not easy. The slant of his left eye tells us that he had more than his share of disappointments in personal relationships and that he expected problems in this area. It also shows a compassion for the suffering of others. From the line that runs from the corner of his mouth onto his chin, we know that in his personal life he suffered great pain and grief. The tension in his chin shows he took life's challenges in stride, steeling himself for the worst.

From the arch on Ben's chin, we can surmise that as a child he was taught that he must be humble, and that it was improper to have a high regard for himself. Unfortunately, this childhood training can leave one with a diminished sense of personal value and a need to over-achieve to prove one's worth. Ben was certainly an over-achiever, but despite his numerous accomplishments, he still needed confirmation of his worth from external sources. In fact, he functioned best when he had at least one source of unquestionable proof of desirability. This face reading insight gives a much more accurate explanation for Ben's need for intimate relationships than what has been written about him.

As you can see, with face reading, you can gain a deeper insight into Ben Franklin's life than history can give us. And the exciting part of revisiting history through face reading is after you have analyzed the picture of a famous historical figure, you can amaze yourself with the accuracy of your insights by looking up their personal biography in any good encyclopedia.

Now, let's try something different. This is a drawing of Ms. Sandra Martin, President of Paraview, Inc. Among many other talents and abilities, Ms. Martin is a successful New York literary agent. Without giving away any more clues, what would you think if you were meeting her for the first time? Remember we are all natural face readers. Before reading further, jot down your immediate first impressions. List everything you think or feel about her. At this point, don't worry about accuracy.

Next check your intuitive feeling against the face reading analysis provided. You may surprise yourself with your natural abilities. The various aspects of the face reading are numbered and each number corresponds to a specific facial feature or grouping. See if you can identify the facial feature that is reflected in the reading. (*The answers are on page 122-123*)

Sandra Martin, President of Paraview, Inc.

1. Ms. Martin's mental focus is people-oriented. She understands and connects with people on a mental level.

2. In her personal life, she sizes up situations quickly and is not afraid to take an opposing point of view.

3. In her professional life, she is a realistic visionary with a dual capability of seeing all the fantastic possibilities and also being able to spot potential problems immediately. She would be best on the planning committee since big ideas are what intrigue her most. By learning to delegate the details she can free up her time for more important matters.

4. A challenge she has with delegation is the fact that she is overly responsible and too hard on herself, especially in her personal life. She tends to figuratively take herself by the collar and force the issue of getting the job done.

5. A natural strategist, she takes in all available information and allows herself time to digest the information as she puts it on her mental framework, then develops a plan. She hates being rushed into making a decision before it feels right to her.

6. Despite strongly developed mental abilities, she operates on an intuitive, almost instinctive level. No matter how good something looks on paper, it has to pass her "gut-check" before she will accept it.

7. With a keen awareness for the appearance of things, she has a real appreciation for beauty.

8. In her work place, she wants her efforts to make a significant difference. She will never do well performing menial tasks or working in an assembly line environment. She needs both to make a major contribution and to connect with people. She is at her best as the owner, manager, or at least a supervisor.

9. She immediately shelters and protects those close to her and those she bonds with.

10. Coming from a space of abundance with a feeling that she has more than enough, including mental, physical, emotional and financial resources, she may nevertheless take on too much and over-tax herself.

11. She has pushed herself too hard. Putting so much focus on the external events in her professional life, she has ignored her own needs for peace, relaxation and joy. In fact, because she pushes so hard, at times she may become uncomfortable in her environment and feel irritable or grumpy.

12. In relationships, Ms. Martin is neither a clinger nor a loner. She can handle intimacy and retain her ability to act independently as well.

13. With a strong libido and an appreciation for physical affections, she is earthy, grounded and has a vital connection with people and with life. She judges people on their abilities, not their gender.

14. She has tremendous reserves of personal energy and power, with a capacity to hang in there for the long haul. Like that famous battery bunny, she can just keep going and going and going.

15. Ms. Martin is not afraid of competition. She feels she is as good as anyone and goes all out for the ideals, goals, and causes she believes in. While she can be tough when needed, she considers the interests and needs of others, too.

16. She is good at organizing and motivating people. Her acceptance of others allows her to gain their cooperation.

17. While she has a natural ability with verbal communication, there are some issues in her personal life that are utterly private.

18. She has developed tremendous courage by facing circumstances that felt totally overwhelming at the time. Her character has been deepened and strengthened by facing and overcoming adversity, and this is especially true in her personal life.

19. She has endured events in her personal life that required her to reach beyond her previous limits. She may have even questioned her ability to survive them, but survive she has and now holds an attitude that she has been tested and can handle anything life may deal her.

20. She sees the broad perspective and is not easily taken in. If something sounds too good to be true, she will be wary about accepting it.

21. She has dealt with disappointments both personally and professionally. In her personal life, it was not just disappointment, but intense loss and pain. Her personal grief has given her a greater empathy and compassion for others.

22. Bonding tightly with those she accepts, she is loyal, faithful and protective of friends and loved ones, but is wary and guarded of all others, especially in the professional world.

23. In her outlook, Ms. Martin is a realist. She is neither overly optimistic nor pessimistic, and is capable of bouncing back from difficulties.

24. A patient listener, she wants to take in all available information.

25. Tenacity is her middle name! Her personal strength and stamina allow her to persist when others would call it quits. This feature also shows loyalty and integrity. When she gives you her word, you can bank on it.

26. She has worked hard at developing her intelligence and broadening her mind, but hides it.

27. She has a natural intuitive ability. She takes in more information than she can process in the moment, but gets intuitive flashes later.

28. Despite her many gifts, she may be an over-achiever, trying to prove her worth. As a child she may not have received enough acknowledgment, or was told it was important to be humble and never brag. As an adult, she needs confirmation of her worth from external sources and especially from at least one other person who provides her with unquestionable proof of her desirability.

29. Gifted with an ability to convince others of her position or point of view, she is a natural promoter.

30. She thinks about and is concerned with money and her own financial security. This may stem from a financially challenged childhood.

The following are the facial features which were the basis for the reading on Sandra Martin. Like the reading of all photographs, this picture of Ms. Martin freezes a moment in time and reflects what is occurring at the moment. Readings in person are easier and more accurate because you can see more aspects of the person, including their smile, teeth, ears, and especially wrinkles and lines that will only show with certain facial expressions.

1. She has *curved eyebrows.*

2. Her *left eyebrow is even* (same thickness throughout) but is also slightly tangled.

3. Her *right eyebrow is winged.* It also has *access hairs* at the start (near the nose). This is a good example of how you can see it on the face when someone has different mental approaches in their personal versus their professional life.

4. She has deep *responsibility lines* running horizontally across the bridge of her nose. She also has strong *forced focus lines* between her eyebrows with the one on her left or personal side slightly deeper and longer.

5. Her *ear/eyebrow combination* is low ears and moderately high eyebrows.

6. While *mental development lines* on the forehead mark mental development, the *prominent inner ear ridges* reflect an even greater connection to internal processes. If you picked up *prescient points*, give yourself extra credit.

7. She has *large earlobes.* Also give yourself credit if you noticed *large nostrils* and a *ball on the end of the nose.* This could be more difficult to see because her nose tip is somewhere between a *small ball* and a *bulb.*

8. If you want to be a leader, just follow your nose. Of course, the bigger the nose the easier it is to follow. She has a *large nose.*

9. Her *wide nose* also says she puts a broad umbrella of support over those she bonds with.

10. *Large nostrils* allow for the free flow of air which is connected with feelings of abundance and generosity. However, like a blacksmith's bellows that stoke a hotter fire, extra large nostrils may cause a person to overestimate their personal resources and take on too much.

11. Her *right eyelid* has a mild or *moderate puff.* (Notice the left eyelid for comparison.) Give yourself credit if you noticed *burn out lines* and *forced focus lines* both of which reflect being too hard on oneself. A personal style or life attitude is usually repeated in several places on the face.

12. Her *left eyelid is thin,* indicating balanced intimacy requirements in her personal life.

13. She has a wide space between the *libido lines* on her upper lip, and they are not strongly defined.

14. A *broad face* with *wide cheeks* reflects her personal style of energy and power. Give yourself extra credit if you also included *big jaws* and *jowls*.

15. Her *chin* is *strong, broad* and *slightly protruding* with a *straight bottom* and *rounded corners* (a blend of straight and round chin).

16. She has *full cheeks*. Connection with people is also reflected in *curved eyebrows* .

17. Gifted with a *large mouth*, she nevertheless has a *secrets line* at the corner of her mouth on the left side.

18. Strongly marked *courage lines* on her cheeks show more prominently on the left.

19. There are *survivor lines* on her upper lip that are more pronounced on the left side.

20. Look for the *big picture lines* at the corners of the eyes that some people call crow's feet. Give yourself credit if you picked up on the *straight bottom lids* which also indicate wariness.

21. She has *disappointment lines* running from her nose to the corners of her mouth. On her personal (left) side, they continue past the corners of her mouth and become *compassion lines*.

22. As noted, she has fairly *straight bottom lids*, however the bottom lid on her professional (right) side is slightly straighter.

23. Her *eyes* don't slant either up or down, so they would be considered *level*.

24. She has *large ears* which also indicate kindness. Notice too, that her *ears* are *low*: the bottoms of her earlobes are lower than her nose. From this observation you could include in her reading that she likes to get things exactly right. Reading her ears as large with low bottoms are both correct readings and not in conflict with each other.

25. Her *big jaws* reflect these qualities. Give yourself credit if you saw a very strong, *broad chin* that slightly sticks out because this also indicates her strength and personal toughness.

26. Her forehead has those *mental development lines* but notice she covers them with her hair.

27. Those little hollow spots at the corners of her eyes are *prescient points*. They work well with her pronounced inner ear ridges.

28. She has a *desirability arch* on her chin.

29. Like Ben Franklin, she has a *thin upper lip* with a *full bottom lip*.

30. As mentioned earlier, her *nose tip* can be read as a *bulb or a small ball*. Better examples of a bulb nose are seen on President Clinton and Karl Malden. Here the reading is as a bulb, but is accurate read both ways.

Sample Readings

Mac Fulfer, author, face reader and attorney

I asked my illustrator, Sandra Williams to do this sample reading of my face. Before she began illustrating the book, I had suggested that she attend my classes and learn face reading in order to understand the internal consistency in faces. She not only learned to read faces, but has been asked many times to give presentations on face reading and to teach what she has learned.

When I shared her reading of me with friends who know me well, their comment was "She nailed you!" All of this is to demonstrate that everyone can learn face reading. It simply requires practice.

The immediate impression I get from Mac's face is that he is rather unconventional and independent with a quick mentality and broad-ranging interests. He's also charming, quite intuitive, and likes people. The other thing I see is that life has held it's challenges for him.

The tangled eyebrows, high bridge to his nose, round full forehead and small, high ears with a backward slant all tell me Mac is unconventional and independent. He would definitely do his best when self-employed because he hates to have anyone looking over his shoulder while he works. He is inner directed and trusts his own counsel.

The full, rounded forehead tells me he is creative in his problem solving, prefers to arrive at his own solutions and won't be held to hard and fast ways of doing things. It is high as well, which says he is quite mental and likes distinctions, wants all the facts and prefers to judge the data himself.

He can be intimidating with his ability to absorb and process information very quickly and immediately express what he has learned, shown by the low, bushy eyebrows and high ears. At the same time, while he might get impatient with slow, plodding situations and people, he'll generally be tactful about how he handles it, indicated by his diplomat ears, large bottom lip (persuasive ability and charm), his round chin (compassionate, acts in terms of people) and support lines (exerts power by exhorting others).

A closer look at his eyebrows and forehead gives further insight into his approach. Not only is he very quick mentally, but his general focus is idea oriented and logical (straight nose). He likes all the pertinent facts as shown by his high forehead, and he prefers the facts be presented quickly (low, nearly straight eyebrows, high ears). He is able to spot potential problems immediately (access hairs) and has a wide range of interests (scattered hairs at the ends of his eyebrows and many mental development lines on his forehead). He is an unconventional thinker who isn't afraid to take an opposing point of view and may play the devil's advocate to gain more information.

Mac is very responsible, drives himself to his limits and cuts himself very little slack. Mental pressure lines diagonally across his forehead plus responsibility lines across the bridge of his nose show his over-responsibility while the freight train line and crooked bottom teeth indicate he sets very high standards and doesn't quit till he's either done or can't move from exhaustion. And that is a likelihood: he has close-set cheeks indicating his energy is quick and intense, not the kind for the long haul. But don't try to stop him: the bump on the bridge of his nose also says he will get feisty if pushed, even for his "own good," plus he has the ability to hang on to his position in the face of opposition (read that as "can be stubborn when necessary") shown by the large front teeth.

On the other hand, Mac can be very persuasive and charming and is a natural promoter, indicated by the lower lip being twice as large as his upper lip. He has the gift of gab and an easy connection with people, note the gab line and the round chin. This is enhanced by tremendous sensitivity shown by the triangle of lines between his eyebrows indicative of a strong right/left brain connection, meaning he's quite intuitive. This is further confirmed by the prescient points beside the inside corners of his eyes and the prominent inner ear ridges.

Mac is open to new information but he will make up his own mind. The small, high ears indicate someone who trusts his own counsel and the down turned mouth means he doesn't necessarily believe what people tell him. With low bushy eyebrows and recessed eyes, he may look laid back, but his mind runs a mile a minute and he will be continually evaluating, turning things over in his mind even if he's nodding yes. That just means he heard you. And yet, he will listen to what people say, wants to hear all the facts and doesn't screen out important information.

In a profile view, Mac's nose is straight and the tip turns up. From that we know that Mac is quite logical, and yet he has the capacity to suspend credulity (upturned tip), allowing him to listen more openly. This softens his skepticism by providing a counterpoint to his down turned mouth, high, small ears and low eyebrows.

He has compassion and concern for others, shown by a number of things: the courage lines across his cheeks and the roundness in his nose tip, cheeks and chin. He has also developed a broader view of life as we can see by the "crow's feet" lines beside his eyes. He is in touch with his own personal power as indicated by his jowls, yet it will generally manifest in actions to help and support others as we can ascertain from both the support lines and round chin. From the lack of prominent ridges on the philtrum we know he generally doesn't stereotype by gender. He judges people on their abilities and inner qualities, not whether they are male or female.

In the personal realm, Mac needs strong connections with people. With some upper eyelids showing, he has balanced intimacy requirements: he is neither a loner nor a clinger. He can share his life with others but he also retains the ability and need to function independently. The wide philtrum (groove beneath the nose) shows a strong libido and a need for physical affection. He is not overtly aggressive as shown by his small, round chin, which combined with the diplomatic ears and support lines, says he would tend to act in terms of people.

The qualities shown in his face of mental acuity, unconventional thinking, wide-ranging interests, sensitivity, and interest in people are a likely mix for an unusual attorney who practices law, reads faces and palms, and interprets dreams.

— *Sandra Williams*

Reading Tips

Whenever you are in doubt about how to read a particular feature, always look at the rest of the face. Each face contains an internal consistency and is its own self-diagnostic. The same type of information will be repeated in several features on the face. The most prominent or pronounced features are the most telling. When you notice a feature but it isn't prominent, you need to soften the reading somewhat. The trait isn't as strong. Think of the characteristics on a scale from one to ten with a ten being the quality expressed to the maximum. A seven or eight on the scale would be not as strong an indication and you would have to soften the reading accordingly. If the feature is a four, five or six, I would suggest you skip it altogether because it is an average feature.

Lines are another matter. If you can see a line, you read it. The deeper, stronger, or longer the line, the greater the significance.

In the third sample reading only some of the major traits were detailed. An in-person reading would be much more extensive. There are many more characteristics that flesh out the depth of Ms. Martin and would be especially obvious if you saw her in person. What it does show is how you can grasp a strong sense of what a person is about and connect with them on that basis from a fairly quick analysis of their major traits. It gets quicker and easier with practice. After several hundred faces, you begin to really see people and their individuality at a glance.

Face reading can change your life because it will change the way you see and understand people. It will allow you to appreciate others on a level you never believed possible. That is the beauty and power of face reading.

SECTION VII — QUICK START

How To Begin Reading Faces

In this section you will actually begin reading faces almost immediately.. Included is an outline of the steps you take to evaluate a face and a worksheet that will help divide the face into its component parts for identification. With this information you can start reading faces, even if you had never heard of face reading before you saw this book.

Step One: Be sure there is enough light to see even the fine lines on the subject's face. Engage the person in conversation. Some revealing features can be seen best as the subject responds. For example, smiles, dimples, and lines are not as easily seen when the person holds a frozen expression.

Step Two: Look at the subject's face at eye level. Be sure their chin is neither up nor down. If the chin is not level, you may get some incorrect readings. For example, if the subject raises his or her chin, it will make the ears appear lower. Conversely, if the chin is lowered, the whites may appear to show under the iris.

Step Three: Notice how light reflects off the subject's face. Look for the most prominent features: those that thrust out into the light, such as a large nose or a strong chin. Also notice which features seem to recede from the light, like recessed eyes. Features that are the most noticeable are the most important. Average features have less meaning and may be difficult to read. A good method to use to determine the importance of a feature is to rate it on a scale from one to ten.

For example, if you are looking at nose size, a very small nose would be a "one" while an extremely large nose would be a "ten." With practice, you can rate every feature. If a nose rated only a "seven" (somewhat large but not extremely so), you would have to soften the reading because it wouldn't have the same importance as a nose that rated a "ten." On the other hand, if you determine the nose rates only "four," "five," or "six," that would indicate that it is an average nose and I would suggest you skip such average features altogether and concentrate on the more outstanding features.

Step Four: Divide the face in half vertically as shown on page 7. Notice all the differences between the left and right sides of the face, including the shapes of eyebrows, eye angles, lines, and dimples. Everything counts, but what is most noticeable counts most. Remember what you see on the subject's left side is about his or her inner world: their personal life, relationships, personal feelings, and maybe even childhood. What you see on the subject's right side reflects attitudes toward their professional or business life and demonstrates their approach to the external world.

Step Five: As you go through the worksheet, you will be able to locate the major areas of the face which are set in bold print, such as Forehead, Eyebrows, Eyes, etc. Below the major feature, you will find the specific type or facial feature with a page number. Match the feature you see on the subject's face with the feature description. For example, if the person's forehead bulges out in the middle, you would check "round and full." If the forehead seems to angle backward from the eyebrows, you would check "backward angle." After you have checked all the facial features that you could identify, look up the page numbers to determine the meanings.

Note: In your first readings, I would suggest looking for the four or five most noticeable features on your subject's face. Even this amount of information will allow you to have a more accurate insight into the subject's personality than you ever imagined. In the Amazing Face Reading classes, I have discovered that the beginning students often focus on the worksheet first, and then try to find that feature on the subject's face. The end result is a worksheet with dozens of checks but many of those checks will have been forced and will not be as accurate as a few checks showing the most outstanding features.

Another common fallacy is to think that the objective in being a good face reader is to be able to spot the tiniest of differences. Occasionally when I have asked a student to tell me the very first thing they notice on a subject's face and they have responded with observations such as, "The left nostril is a little larger than the right one," I am always amused by such a response, especially when the subject may have incredible eyebrows, a large chin, or ears that stick straight out. In face reading, what you are looking for is not the minutia but those features you couldn't possibly miss.

I developed the worksheets for my classes to give students an easy format to begin reading faces immediately. If you need additional worksheets, please use the order form at the back of the book.

Checklist

1. Forehead
- ❏ Round and full
  (forehead protrudes forward) [11]
- ❏ Backward angle
  (forehead slopes back) [11]
- ❏ Straight
  (forehead is straight up) [11]
- ❏ Self-will pad
  (fleshy bump between eyebrows) [12]
- ❏ Brow ridge
  (a bony ridge above eyes) [12]
- ❏ No brow ridge
  (no bony ridge above the eyes) [12]

2. Eyebrows
- ❏ Curved
  (smooth curve) [13]
- ❏ Straight
  (no curve or angle) {13]
- ❏ Angled
  (definite up and down) [13]
- ❏ High
  (wide space between eye and eyebrow) [14]
- ❏ Low
  (no space between eye and eyebrow) [14]
- ❏ Bushy
  (thick, full eyebrow hairs) [15]
- ❏ Thin
  (like a pencil line) [15]
- ❏ Winged
  (thick at beginning, thinning at ends) [15]
- ❏ Even
  (same thickness throughout length) [15]
- ❏ Managerial
  (thin at beginning, thick at outer edges) [15]
- ❏ Continuous
  (both eyebrows connected) [16]
- ❏ Tangled
  (eyebrow hairs tangled) [16]
- ❏ Access hairs
  (hairs growing straight up at beginning) [16]
- ❏ Scattered hairs
  (single hairs at outsides of eyebrows) [16]
- ❏ Chameleon
  (nearly invisible eyebrows) [16]

3. Eyes
- ❏ Widely spaced
  (more than one eye's width apart) [17]
- ❏ Closely spaced
  (less than one eye's width apart) [17]
- ❏ Angles up
  (outer corner higher than inner corner) [18]
- ❏ Angles down
  (outer corner lower than inner corner) [18]
- ❏ No angle
  (inner and outer corners on a level line) [18]
- ❏ Bulging
  (eyes appear to bulge out of sockets) [19]
- ❏ Recessed
  (eyes are deep in sockets) [19]
- ❏ Large full iris
  (seems to fill the eye) [20]
- ❏ Small iris
  (small in relation to the eyeball) [20]
- ❏ Prescient points
  (BB-size indents at inside corner of eyes) [20]
- ❏ Stressed
  (white showing below iris) [22]
- ❏ Violent
  (white showing above iris) [22]
- ❏ Disconnected
  (white showing all around iris) [22]

4. Eyelids
- ❏ Abundant lids
  (most of upper lid is visible) [23]
- ❏ Thin lids
  (some of upper lid is showing) [23]
- ❏ No lids
  (no upper lid showing) [23]
- ❏ Straight
  (bottom lids straight) [24]
- ❏ Curved
  (bottom lids are curved) [24]
- ❏ Round
  (bottom lids are very round) [25]

5. Eye puffs
- ❏ Moderate
  (skin above eye has extra folds) [26]
- ❏ Intense
  (skin above eye hangs down over eye) [26]

6. Nose
- ❏ Large
  (in proportion to whole face) [27]
- ❏ Long
  (from between eyes to nose tip) [27]
- ❏ Short
  (in proportion to whole face) [27]
- ❏ Long and straight
  (when viewed in profile) [28]
- ❏ Concave
  ("ski slope" in profile) [28]
- ❏ Arched
  (curves out viewed in profile) [28]
- ❏ Bump on bridge
  (nose widens below bridge) [28]
- ❏ No ridge
  (no pronounced bridge) [29]
- ❏ High ridge
  (pronounced bridge) [29]
- ❏ High, wide ridge
  (straight from forehead with no indent) [29]
- ❏ Wide
  (wide at base) [30]
- ❏ Thin
  (nose appears to be pinched) [30]
- ❏ Crease
  (on flange) [30]
- ❏ Groove
  (deeper line on flange) [30]

7. Nose Tip
- ❏ Turns up
  (angles up in profile) [31]
- ❏ No angle
  (horizontal in profile) [31]
- ❏ Turns down
  (angles down in profile) [32]
- ❏ Turns down and pointed
  (down turned with sharp tip) [32]
- ❏ Big bulb
  (bulb on end of nose) [32]
- ❏ Small ball
  (at tip of nose) [33]
- ❏ Skinny tip
  (thin or pinched tip) [33]

Nose tip continued
- ❑ Groove
  (groove or dimple in tip) [33]
- ❑ Heart-shaped
  (flaccid tip hangs down [33]

8. Nostrils
- ❑ Very small *[34]*
- ❑ Very large *[34]*
- ❑ Long, narrow *[34]*
- ❑ Huge, flared *[34]*
- ❑ Round *[35]*
- ❑ Rectangular *[35]*
- ❑ Small, triangular *[35]*
- ❑ Low septum
  (divider between nostrils) [35]

9. Ears
- ❑ Large
  (in proportion to head) [36]
- ❑ Small
  (in proportion to head) [36]
- ❑ Prominent outer cups
  (outside rim of cartilage) [37]
- ❑ Prominent inner cups
  (inner ring of raised cartilage) [37]
- ❑ Parallel angle
  (vertical) [38]
- ❑ Pronounced angle
  (slants backwards) [38]
- ❑ Stick out
  (away from head) [39]
- ❑ Close to head
  (almost touch head) [39]
- ❑ Diplomat
  (tops close to head, bottoms stick out) [39]
- ❑ High tops
  (tops are as high or higher than eyes) [40]
- ❑ Low bottoms
  (ear lobes are as low as or lower than bottom of nose) [40]

10. Ear/Eyebrow Combinations
- ❑ High ears/high eyebrows *[41]*
- ❑ High ears/low eyebrows *[41]*
- ❑ Low ears/high eyebrows *[41]*
- ❑ Low ears/low eyebrows *[41]*

11. Cheeks
- ❑ Protruding
  (movie star) [42]
- ❑ Full
  (rounded with no bones showing) [42]
- ❑ Narrow
  (close together) [42]
- ❑ Wide
  (set far apart) [43]
- ❑ Sunken
  (drawn and flaccid) [43]
- ❑ Healer
  (broadest at sides, beside eyes) [43]

12. Mouth
- ❑ Large
  (in proportion to face) [44]
- ❑ Small
  (in proportion to face) [44]
- ❑ Turns up
  (corners higher than middle) [45]
- ❑ Straight
  (forms straight line) [45]
- ❑ Turns down
  (corners lower than middle) [45]

13. Lips
- ❑ Full
  (both lips large and full) [46]
- ❑ Full lower
  (bottom much larger than upper) [46]
- ❑ Full upper
  (upper much larger than lower) [46]
- ❑ Thin
  (may appear as a thin line) [47]
- ❑ Cupid's bow
  (upper looks like a cupid's bow) [47]

14. Teeth
- ❑ Even
  (all same length) [48]
- ❑ Gap
  (space between two front teeth) [48]
- ❑ Big front teeth
  (hang down longer than other teeth) [48]
- ❑ Crooked
  (especially bottom teeth) [48]
- ❑ Buck teeth
  (front teeth protrude) [48]

15. Smiles
- ❑ Natural
  (lips relaxed, teeth show, but no gums) [49]
- ❑ Gums show
  (in a full smile) [49]
- ❑ Stretched tight
  (upper lip tight across teeth) [49]
- ❑ Crooked
  (one side higher than the other) [49]

16. Jaws
- ❑ Big
  (stick out when seen from behind) [50]
- ❑ Narrow
  (face is thin at jaws) [50]
- ❑ Jowls
  (pads of flesh hang from jawline) [50]
- ❑ Ripples
  (pumping jaw muscle) [50]

17. Chins
- ❑ Strong *[51]*
- ❑ Sticks out *[51]*
- ❑ Broad *[51]*
- ❑ Very broad *[52]*
- ❑ Long *[52]*
- ❑ Small *[52]*
- ❑ Receding
  (mouth protrudes more than chin [53]
- ❑ Round *[53]*
- ❑ Straight *[53]*
- ❑ Pointed *[54]*
- ❑ Very pointed *[54]*

18. Chin/Eyebrow Combinations
- ❑ Round chin/curved eyebrows *[55]*
- ❑ Round chin/straight eyebrows *[55]*
- ❑ Round chin/angled eyebrows *[55]*
- ❑ Straight chin/curved eyebrows *[56]*
- ❑ Straight chin/straight eyebrows *[56]*
- ❑ Straight chin/angled eyebrows *[56]*
- ❑ Pointed chin/curved eyebrows *[57]*
- ❑ Pointed chin/straight eyebrows *[57]*
- ❑ Pointed chin/angled eyebrows *[57]*

19. Dimples and Clefts

- ❑ Good sport
  (dimple in chin) [60]
- ❑ Adaptability cleft
  (cleft in chin) [60]
- ❑ Destiny
  (dimple in tip of nose) [60]
- ❑ Romantic dimple
  (dimple in one or both cheeks [60]

20. Lines

- ❑ Mental development
  (horizontal lines on forehead) [61]
- ❑ Mental pressure
  (diagonal lines on forehead) [61]
- ❑ Freight train
  (single deep line between eyebrows) [61]
- ❑ Forced focus
  (two lines between eyebrows) [62]
- ❑ Perfectionist
  (more than two lines between eyebrows) [62]
- ❑ Visionary
  (triangle between eyebrows) [62]
- ❑ Burn-out
  (deep horizontal line on bridge of nose) [62]
- ❑ Responsibility
  (many fine lines on bridge of nose) [63]
- ❑ Big Picture
  (crow's feet at corners of eyes) [63]
- ❑ Courage
  (diagonal lines across cheek bones) [63]
- ❑ Humor
  (on sides of nose) [63]
- ❑ Disappointment
  (nose to corner of mouth) [64]
- ❑ Compassion
  (corner of mouth to chin) [64]
- ❑ Forced smile
  (horizontal line above upper lip) [64]
- ❑ Support
  (dimples that look like lines) [64]
- ❑ Libido
  (vertical ridges under nose) [65]
- ❑ Survivor
  (vertical lines on upper lip) [65]
- ❑ Gab
  (continuous line runs under chin) [65]
- ❑ Desirability
  (arch on chin) [65]

- ❑ Heart
  (vertical line on ear lobe) [66]
- ❑ Secrets
  (indents at corners of mouth) [66]
- ❑ Obstinate chin
  (chin has a tense, bumpy appearance) [66]

21. Facial Hair

- ❑ Mustache *[67]*
- ❑ Round beard *[67]*
- ❑ Square beard *[68]*
- ❑ Pointed beard *[68]*

22. Face Shape

- ❑ Broad
  (wide, square face) [70]
- ❑ Narrow
  (thin or long face) [70]
- ❑ Diamond
  (wide at cheeks, narrow at chin) [70]
- ❑ Pear-shaped
  (broadest under chin) [71]
- ❑ Flat
  (no features protrude) [71]

23. Face Types

- ❑ Mental
  (thin face, large forehead, small chin/jaw) [72]
- ❑ Physical
  (large, square face, big jaws and chin) [72]
- ❑ Emotional
  (round face and chin, full cheeks) [72]

24. Combination Face Types

- ❑ Mental/physical
  (broad forehead, square chin) [73]
- ❑ Mental/emotional
  (high, broad forehead, round chin) [73]
- ❑ Physical/emotional
  (square face, round chin) [73]

25. Facial Dominance

- ❑ Large upper
  (from hairline to eyebrows) [74]
- ❑ Large middle
  (from eyebrows to bottom of nose) [74]
- ❑ Large lower
  (from bottom of nose to bottom of chin) [74]
- ❑ Small upper
  (forehead is smallest area) [75]

- ❑ Small middle
  (nose area is smallest) [75]
- ❑ Small lower
  (chin area is smallest) [75]

26. Profile Types

- ❑ Convex
  (forehead angles back, nose most forward) [76]
- ❑ Extremely convex
  (prominent nose, extreme angle to chin and forehead) [76]
- ❑ Moderately convex
  (mild angle to forehead and chin) [76]
- ❑ Concave
  (full forehead, protruding chin) [77]
- ❑ Extreme concave
  (dish-shaped profile) [77]
- ❑ Balanced
  (neither convex nor concave) [77]
- ❑ Convex/concave
  (forehead slants back, chin protrudes) [78]
- ❑ Concave/convex
  (forehead full, chin recedes) [78]

27. Head Types

- ❑ High crown/low forehead
  (highest point at crown) [79]
- ❑ High forehead/low crown
  (highest point at hairline) [79]
- ❑ Round
  (viewed from behind) [80]
- ❑ Square
  (viewed from behind) [80]

Suggested Reading

The Naked Face, Lailan Young, 1993

Frogs into Princes, Neuro Linguistic Programming Richard Bandler and John Ginder, 1979

Your Face Never Lies, What Your Face Reveals About You and Your Health, an Introduction to Oriental Diagnosis, Michio Kushi, 1983

Getting in T-Touch, Understand and Influence Your Horse's Personality, Linda Tellington-Jones with Sybil Taylor, 1995

About Faces, The Evolution of the Human Face, Terry Landau, 1989

Emotional Intelligence, Daniel Goleman , 1995

Aiken, Pauline. "Arcite's Illness and Vincent of Beauvals," PMLA, LI (1936) 361-9

_____. "The Summoner's Malady," SP, XXXIII (1936), 40-4

_____. "Vincent of Beauvais and Dame Pertelote's Knowledge of Medicine," Speculum, X (1935), 28l-7

Aristotle. Historia Animalium. Vol. IV of The Works of Aristotle. Edited by J. A. Smith and W. D. Ross and translated by D'Arcy Wentworth Thompson. London: Oxford University Press, 1910

_____. "Physiognomics," Minor Works. Edited by T. E. Page, E. Capps, and W. H. D. Rouse and translated by W. S. Hett. Cambridge, Massachusetts: Harvard University Press, 1936.

_____. "Physiognomonica," Opuscula. Vol VI of The Works of Aristotle. Edited by W .D. Ross and translated by T. Loveday and E. S. Forster. Oxford: Clarendon Press, 1913.

Barrow, Sarah F. The Medieval Society Romances. New York: Columbia University Press, 1924.

Baum, Paull F. "Chaucer's Puns," PMLA, LXXI (1956), 242-5.

Beichner, Paul E. "Daun Piers, Monk and Business Administration," Speculum, XXXIV (1959), 611-9.

Bloomfield, Morton W. "Chaucer's Summoner and the Girls of the Diocese," PQ, XXXVIII (1949), 503-7.

Bowden, Muriel. A commentary on the General Prologue to the Canterbury Tales. New York: The Macmillan Company, 1957.

Brown, J. Wood. An Enquiry into the Life and Legend of Michael Scot. Edinburgh: David Douglas, 1897.

Clark, Thomas. "Forehead of Chaucer's Prioress," PQ, IX (1930), 312-4.

Curry, Walter Clyde. Chaucer and the Mediaeval Sciences. New York: Oxford University Press, 1926.

_____. "Chaucer's Science and Art," Texas Review, VIII (July, 1923), 307-22.

_____. The Middle English Ideal of Personal Beauty. Baltimore: J.H. Furst Company, 1916

_____. "The Secret of Chaucer's Pardoner," JEGP, XVIII (1919), 593-606.

Cutts, Edward L. Scenes and Characters of the Middle Ages. London: Simkin, Marshall, Hamilton, Kent & Company, 1926.

Davis, R. T. "Chaucer's Madame Eglentine," MLN, LXVII (1952), 400-2.

Dodd, William George. Courtly Love in Chaucer and Gower. Gloucester, Mass.: Peter Smith, 1959.

Emerson, Oliver Farrar. "Some of Chaucer's Lines on the Monk," MP, I (1903), 105-15.

Gaster, M. ed. "The Hebrew Version of the 'Secretum Secretorum.'" Journal of the Royal Asiatic Society of Great Britain and Ireland (1908), 111-62 and 1065 - 84.

Greenhill, William Alexander. Dictionary of Greek and Roman Biography and Mythology. Vol. III. Edited by William Smith. London: James Walton, 1870.

Gunn, Alan M.F. The Mirror of Love. Lubbock, Texas: Texas Tech Press, 1952.

Haselmayer, Louis A. "The Apparitor and Chaucer's Summoner," Speculum, XII (1937), 43-57.

_____. "Chaucer and Medieval Verse Portraiture." Unpublished Ph. D. dissertation, Department of English, Yale University, 1937.

Kirby, Thomas A. Chaucer's Triolus. Baton Rouge: Louisana State University, 1940.

Kittredge, George Lyman. Chaucer and His Poetry. 11th ed. Cambridge, Mass., Harvard University Press, 1956.

Krapp, George Philip. "Chaucer's Triolus and Criseyde," PQ, XVII (1938), 235.

Kuhl, E. P. "Chaucer's Madame Eglantine," MLN, LX (1945), 325-6.

Lacroix, Paul. Science and Literature in the Middle Ages. London: Bickers and Son, n. d.

Lewis, O. S. The Allegory of Love. London: Geoffrey Cumberlege, 1936.

Lowes, John Livingston. "The Art of Geoffrey Chaucer," Essays in Appreciation. Boston: Houghton Mifflin Company, 1936.

Lumiansky, R. M. Of Sondry Folk. Austin: University of Texas Press, 1955.

Lydgate and Burgh. Secrees of Old Philosoffres. Vol. LXVI of EETS, Extra Series. Edited by Robert Steele. London: Kegan Paul, Trench, Trubner & Co., 1894.

Lynch, James J. "The Prioress's Greatest Oath, Once More," MLN, LXII (1957), 242-9.

Madeleva, Sister M. A Lost Language. New York: Sheed and Ward, 1951.

Manly, John Matthews, ed. Canterbury Tales. New York: Henry Holt and Company, 1926.

_____. Some New Light on Chaucer. New York: Peter Smith, 1951.

Metham, Joh. "Physiognomy," The works of John Metham. Vol CXXXII of EETS, Original Series. Edited by Hardin Craig. London: Kegan Paul, Trench, Trubner & Co., Ltd., 1916.

Additional Physiognomy References

Moore, Authur K. "The Eyen Greye of Chaucer's Prioress," PQ, XXVI (1947), 307-12.

Morris, William. "Preface," Medieval Lore from Bartholomew Anglicus. London: Chatto & Windus, 1924.

A New English Dictionary of Historical Principles. Edited by Sir James A. H. Murray. Oxford: Clarendon Press, 1909.

"Physiognomy," Vol XXI of Encyclopaedia Britannica. 11th ed. Cambridge, England: University Press, 1911.

"Physiognomy," Vol XIX of Encyclopaedia Britannica. 9th ed. Chicago: R. S. Peale & Co., 1890.

Plimpton, George A. The Education of Chaucer. London: Oxford Universtiy Press, 1935.

Power, Eileen. "Madame Eglentyne," Medieval People. New York: Barnes & Noble, Inc., 1924.

Rickert, Edith. Chaucer's World. New York: Columbia University Press, 1948.

Robin, P. Ansell. The Old Physiology in English Literature. New York: E. P. Dutton & Co., 1911.

Robinson, F. N., ed. The Works of Geoffrey Chaucer. 2d ed. Boston: Houghton Mifflin Company, 1957.

Root Robert Kilburn. "Chaucer's Cares," MP, XV (1917), 1-22.

Sarton, George. Introduction to the History of Science. 3 vols. Baltimore: The Williams & Wilkins Company, 1927-48.

Saunders, Richard. Physiognomie, and Chiromancie, Metoposcopie. 2d ed. London: H. Brugis, 1671.

Seligman, Kurt. The History of Magic. Wakefield, Mass.: The Murray Printing Company, 1948.

Steadman, John M. "The Prioress' Dog and Benedictine Discipline," MP, LIV (1956), 1-6.

Steele, Robert, ed. Medieval Lore from Bartholomew Anglicus. London: Chatto & Windus, 1924.

_____. ed. Secrees of Old Philosoffrees. Vol. LXVI of EETS, Extra Series. London: Kegan Paul, Trench, Trubner & Co., 1894.

Steele, Robert, ed. Secretus Secretorum. London: Oxford University Press, 1920.

Tatlock, John S. P. and Arthus G. Kennedy. A Concordance to the Complete Works of Geoffrey Chaucer. Washington: The Carnegie Institute of Washington, 1927.

Thorndike, Lynn. "Buridan's Questions on the Physiognomy Ascribed to Aristotle," Speculum, XVIII (January, 1943), 99-103.

_____. A History of Magic and Experimental Science. Vols. 1 and 2. New York: The Macmillan Company. 1923.

_____. A History of Magic and Experimental Science. Vol. VI. New York: Columbia University Press, 1941.

Three Prose Versions of the Secreta Secretorum. Vol. LXXIV of EETS, Extra Series. Edited by Robert Steele. London: Kegan Paul, Trench, Trubner & Co., 1898.

Wainwright, Benjamin B. "Chaucer's Prioress Again: An Interpretative Note,: MLN, XLVIII (1933), 34-7.

Willard, Rudolph. "Chaucer's 'Text that Seith that Hunters Ben Nat Hooly Men.'" Studies in English. Austin: The University of Texas Press, 1947.

The Works of Geoffrey Chaucer, 2d ed. Edited by F. N. Robinson. Boston: Houghton Mifflin Company, 1957.

Wright, Thomas. "Preface," De Regimine Principum. Quoted in Hoocleve's Works, Minor Poems. Vol LXI of EETS, Extra Series. London: Oxford University Press, 1937.

Young, Karl. "The 'Secree of Secrees' of Chaucer's Canon's Yeoman," MLN, LVIII (1943), 98-105.

Order Form

To order additional copies of *Amazing Face Reading*:

Telephone Orders:

Call The Rainbow Bridge: (817) 377-2001. Have your AMEX, Optima, Discover, VISA or MasterCard ready.

Postal Orders mail to:

(Make checks payable to Mac Fulfer)

Mac Fulfer
P. O. Box 100904
Ft. Worth, TX 76185

Quantity	Total	
Books _____ @ $17.95 each	$_____	
Sales Tax *(TX residents only)*$1.48/bk	$_____	
Shipping *(See at right.)*	$_____	
Total	$_____	

Send to — Please Print

Name _____

Address _____ Apt. No._____

City _____ State _____ Zip _____

Phone: Work (_____)_____ Home (_____)_____

For information about Face Reading Classes, Presentations, Seminars and Jury Selections, Call 1 (800) 697-6096 or
(817) 336-3445 or (817) 737-6934
Email: FaceReadng@aol.com
Website: amazingfacereading.com

Order Information:

Price: $17.95 each.

Sales tax: Texas residents add 8.25% to total cost of books. ($1.48/book)

Shipping (within the USA)
One or two books: $3.20 (No additional shipping charges to same address.) Three or four books: $6.40 (to same address).

For orders outside USA, call (800)697-6096

Order Form

To order additional copies of *Amazing Face Reading*:

Telephone Orders:

Call The Rainbow Bridge: (817) 377-2001. Have your AMEX, Optima, Discover, VISA or MasterCard ready.

Postal Orders mail to:

(Make checks payable to Mac Fulfer)

Mac Fulfer
P. O. Box 100904
Ft. Worth, TX 76185

Quantity	Total	
Books _____ @ $17.95 each	$_____	
Sales Tax *(TX residents only)*$1.48/bk	$_____	
Shipping *(See at right.)*	$_____	
Total	$_____	

Send to — Please Print

Name _____

Address _____ Apt. No._____

City _____ State _____ Zip _____

Phone: Work (_____)_____ Home (_____)_____

For information about Face Reading Classes, Presentations, Seminars and Jury Selections, Call 1 (800) 697-6096 or
(817) 336-3445 or (817) 737-6934
Email: FaceReadng@aol.com
Website: amazingfacereading.com

Order Information:

Price: $17.95 each.

Sales tax: Texas residents add 8.25% to total cost of books. ($1.48/book)

Shipping (within the USA)
One or two books: $3.20 (No additional shipping charges to same address.) Three or four books: $6.40 (to same address).

For orders outside USA, call (800)697-6096